The Faiths of Our Fathers

The FAITHS of Our FATHERS

WHAT AMERICA'S FOUNDERS REALLY BELIEVED

ALF J. MAPP, JR.

ROWMAN & LITTLEFIELD PUBLISHERS, INC.

Lanham Boulder New York Oxford

*To my wife, Ramona Hartley Mapp,
and my son, Alf Johnson Mapp III*

ROWMAN & LITTLEFIELD PUBLISHERS, INC.

Published in the United States of America by Rowman & Littlefield Publishers, Inc.
A wholly owned subsidary of the Rowman & Littlefield Publishing Group, Inc.
4501 Forbes Boulevard, Suite 200, Lanham, Maryland 20706
www.rowmanlittlefield.com

PO Box 317
Oxford
OX2 9RU, UK

Distributed by National Book Network

British Library Cataloguing in Publication Information Available

Library of Congress Cataloging-in-Publication Data

Mapp, Alf J. (Alf Johnson), 1925–
The faiths of our fathers : what America's founders really believed / Alf J. Mapp, Jr.
p. cm.
Includes bibliographical references (p.) and index.
1. Statesmen—United States—Biography. 2. Statesmen—Religious life—United
States—History—18th century. 3. Presidents—United States—Biography. 4.
Presidents—Religious life—United States—History—18th century. 5. United States—
Politics and government—1775–1783. 6. United States—Religion—To 1800. 7. Religion
and politics—United States—History—18th century. 8. Freedom of religion—United
States—History—18th century. I. Title.
E302.5.M26 2003
270.7'092'273—dc21   2003008790

ISBN: 978-0-7425-3115-4

Printed in the United States of America

Contents

CONTENTS

Acknowledgments

Among the institutions whose helpfulness has made this book possible are the Library of Congress, Washington, D.C.; the Alderman Library of the University of Virginia; the Sween Library of the College of William and Mary; the Old Dominion University Library; the Library of the University of North Carolina; the Tidewater Community College Library; the Library of Virginia in Richmond; the University of Richmond Library; and the Portsmouth, Va., Public Library System, especially the gracious and efficient staff of the Churchland Branch, and of these especially its resourceful and indefatigable director of interlibrary loans, Jeanette Toms.

With full cooperation of the administration, Melba Meador obtained permission for me to visit Charles Carroll's home at a time when normally it would be closed to the public. She also obtained permission for me to photocopy a picture of Carroll in the Maryland Archives.

Special thanks are due individuals who shared their expertise. I profited from conversations with Bernard Bailyn of Harvard University, twice the winner of Pulitzer prizes for writing on American history; Paul C. Nagel, whose books on the Adamses have made John, Abigail, and John Quincy live again for many Americans; Kenneth W. Thompson, the University of Virginia's famous expert on American presidents; Mary Washington College's Daniel Preston, editor of the James Monroe papers; William and Mary's Charles F. Hobson, editor of the John Marshall papers and one of the best in the whole canon of Marshall biographers; Martin E. Marty, the Chicago savant who is perhaps the greatest historian of religion in America; and Ronald Hofmann, the biographer who has resuscitated Charles Carroll of Carrollton and made him better known to many Americans today than he was to most of his contemporaries. I have enjoyed the counsel of some of the world's foremost scholars in their specialties.

I am grateful to my technology assistant, Jeanne King, and communications facilitator, Donald King, who have made my work much easier. Charlene Mudrock efficiently maintains the website that keeps me in touch with readers and potential readers.

I appreciate the intelligence, courtesy, and respect for craftsmanship of publisher Jon Sisk; his assistant, Sally Mays; and production editor Lynn Weber.

Ultimately I am grateful to my wife, Ramona Hartley Mapp, to whom I have dedicated five previous volumes, and to my son, Alf Johnson Mapp III. They were the first audience for many portions of this book, and Alf was an eagle-eyed reader of the printer's proofs.

Frontispiece: Inauguration of Washington. Courtesy of the Library of Congress.

Chapter 1: George Washington. Courtesy of the Library of Congress.

Chapter 2: Thomas Jefferson, oil painting, by Rembrant Peale, 1805. © Collection of the New York Historical Society.

Chapter 3: Benjamin Franklin. Courtesy of the Franklin Collection, Yale University Library.

Chapter 4: James Madison, miniature portrait by Charles Wilson Peale. Courtesy of the Library of Congress.

Chapter 5: John Adams. Courtesy of the Library of Congress.

Chapter 6: George Washington. Courtesy of the Bailey Art Museum, University of Virginia.

Chapter 7: John Marshall. Courtesy of the Virginia Historical Society.

Chapter 8: Patrick Henry. Courtesy of Dementi Photo, by permission of the Speaker of the Virginia House of Delegates.

Chapter 9: Alexander Hamilton, by John Trumbull. Courtesy of the Library of Congress.

Chapter 10: George Mason. Courtesy of George Mason University.

Chapter 11: Charles Carroll of Carrollton. Courtesy of Maryland State Archives.

Chapter 12: Haym Salomon and friends. Courtesy of Jacob Rader Marcus Center of the American Jewish Archives, Cincinnati Campus, Hebrew Union College Jewish Institute of Religion.

1

In the Beginning Was Variety

PERHAPS it should not be surprising that a time such as ours, with markedly increased interest in America's Founding Fathers and in religion, has spawned many questions about the religion of the nation's early patriots.

Some questioners seek enlightenment from the thoughts of some of America's best minds. Others seek increased understanding of prominent molders of our culture. Still others approach the question in the spirit of choosing sides in a contest, wanting to claim the most outstanding players for their team whether it be fundamentalist or atheist, or something between.

There was no monolithic national faith acknowledged by all

Founding Fathers. Their religious attitudes were as varied as their political opinions.

Even one who has spent many years in researching the era of the Founders finds some surprises. One famous political leader generally regarded as a red-hot radical became essentially a fundamentalist. Another famed for common sense and hard-headed realism viewed creation as composed of many solar systems, each with its own God. One celebrated for conventional piety created a mystery by refusing to take communion. One of the most prominent Founders, a man popularly regarded as materialistic and dissolute, attempted to found an organization of Christian conservatives to promote the election to political office of "like-minded men."

Searching for the truth about the attitudes toward religion of such an influential, and in many cases brilliant group, has helped me to gain a better understanding of my native land. I have also found it a fascinating pursuit. I hope you will too.

2

Thomas Jefferson

WHEN Thomas Jefferson attended church services as an old man, tears would spring to his eyes at the sound of familiar hymns. The sight would have been startling to those New England ministers who warned during his first presidential campaign that, if Jefferson were elected, he would confiscate all Bibles and convert churches into temples of prostitution.

Admittedly, the tears may have been inspired more by nostalgia than by religious emotion. When Jefferson was a young boy, he had sung those songs with his beloved sister Jane by the family fireside in winter and on the banks of the Rivanna River in the "soft summer twilight." Three years his senior, she had been his constant companion and his instructor in many things. He always maintained that her understanding had been the equal of his own. Young as she was, she partially filled a maternal role. Tom was one of ten children born to Mrs. Jefferson within a period of fifteen years, the middle child of five born within six years. She was pregnant roughly four and a half of the first ten years of Tom's life.

Mrs. Jefferson nevertheless found time to teach her young son some prayers. He remembered childhood days when he recited the Lord's Prayer for company at dinner. He seems to have been brought up in the rituals and customs of the Anglican Church as it existed in colonial Virginia, for the most part less of a high church institution than its English counterpart.

Tom's father, Peter Jefferson, was a member of the House of Burgesses and an all-around leading citizen of the mountain county he called home. Without the benefit of a college education, a scarce commodity on the frontier, he had acquired a rich fund of knowledge from wide reading. He and his associate, Colonel Joshua Fry, were recognized as the foremost cartographers in North America in their day. Tom loved to hear his father tell of adventures on wilderness expeditions that included parleying with Indians, escaping an angry bear, and sleeping in a hollow tree. Peter Jefferson was his son's great hero. His father's death when Tom was fourteen was one of the great traumas of his life.

At age sixteen, he asked the guardian of his estate for permission to go off to college. Tom argued that the move would save money, since his presence at home drew a constant swarm of friends who stayed for dinner. At the College of William and Mary, he was strongly impressed with the intelligence of some of his professors, especially George Wythe, a man as notable for charm as intellect, and William Small, who he later said "probably fixed the destinies of my life."

With Williamsburg itself, he was not so favorably impressed. Seeing it as a den of drunkards, gamblers, and sexual libertines, he called it Devilsburg. Years later, he recollected,

I had the good fortune to become acquainted very early with some characters of very high standing, and to feel the incessant wish that I could ever become what they were. Under temptations and difficulties, I would ask myself—what would Dr. Small, Mr. Wythe, [Cousin] Peyton Randolph do in this situation? What course is it will assure me their approbation? I am certain that this mode of deciding on my conduct tended more to correctness than any reasoning power I possessed. Knowing the even and dignified line they pursued, I could never doubt for a moment which of two courses would be in character for them, whereas, seeking the same object through a process of moral reasoning, and with the jaundiced eye of youth, I should have often erred.

Available evidence suggests that, as a college student, Jefferson was well-behaved and diligent. He avoided the fleshpots of Devilsburg and was often hard at work with his studies when a roistering fellow student, returning from a night on the town, upset Tom's table of books. But young Jefferson was not kept on the narrow path by Bible lessons. When confronted by temptation, he did not ask, "What would Jesus do?" Instead, he imitated the behavior of respected members of the society in which he lived.

Jefferson's belief that Professor Small had "probably fixed the destinies of my life" rested on the fact that the Scottish-born professor introduced the youth to the philosophy of the Enlightenment. The Scottish Enlightenment, of which the teacher was a product, was an intellectual movement ultimately at least as influential as its more famous French counterpart. Its concern with individual rights, the rule of reason, and human capacity for self-improvement and self-government would find its way into many of America's most cherished state documents, including the Declaration of Independence.

Small's influence on Jefferson was reinforced by the fact that, impressed with his student's native genius, he made him his daily companion. He introduced him to the works of Francis Bacon,

Isaac Newton, and John Locke, who became, and remained, the young man's favorite heroes. Small brought to Jefferson the Enlightenment's questioning attitude toward all institutions. All of Jefferson's previous teachers had been Anglican clergymen, a group not noted for skepticism, particularly in regard to the Establishment.

The young man's skill as a fiddler carried him to the Governor's Palace as an entertainer, but his ability as a conversationalist earned him many future invitations. With Professors Small and Wythe, he spent many hours in conversation with Governor Francis Fauquier, a sophisticated intellectual appointed to colonial office to rescue him from gambling debts in England. Fauquier may have encouraged Jefferson in skepticism, but the reports of the Governor's gambling problems had a conservative moral influence. Jefferson developed such a horror of gambling that, as a father and grandfather, he would not permit card-playing in his home.

The skepticism that Jefferson absorbed as a teenager caused him to question not only accepted political institutions of the day but also the church and even religion itself. There is no evidence that he became an atheist. After all, he was trying to follow the dictates of logic, and no one has ever found a logical proof for atheism. But he probably did become an agnostic.

He read hungrily in philosophy, history, and science, devouring works in English, Greek, Latin, and French. At some point, agnosticism yielded to faith. But his beliefs were still nebulous. The one point of consistency was his adherence to Christian ethics.

Deism was the theology dominant among intellectuals in the English-speaking world, and he doubtless considered himself a Deist. He believed that the existence of creation presupposed a creator. He was disposed to believe that the creator was just, probably even benevolent. From various sources, but particularly from the writings of the Deist philosopher Henry St. John, Viscount Bolingbroke, he derived the conviction that no mystical revelation would provide the answers to his questions. Reason would be his only dependable guide.

Such were Jefferson's somewhat nebulous ideas about religion when he became an attorney at the age of twenty-four and when he was elected to the Virginia legislature two years later. The fact that Jefferson as a legislator supported the call for a day of prayer when revolution neared is sometimes cited as evidence that he believed in the efficacy of petitions to the Almighty. But we cannot know whether his action was prompted by such a belief or solely by the desire to promote unity and raise public morale.

When Jefferson became the principal author of the Declaration of Independence in 1776, he asserted the right of the United States to "assume the separate and equal station to which the Laws of Nature and Nature's God entitle them." This was in accord with his intention to express the consensus of the Congress in terms and concepts acceptable to the members. He was not striving for originality.

The document concluded, "And for the support of this declaration, with a firm reliance on the protection of divine Providence, we mutually pledge to each other our lives, our fortunes, and our sacred honor." The statement was an expression of faith by a group of men self-conscious about using the word "God." There is no reason to doubt that most of them, including Jefferson, were sincere in both their dedication and their restraint. When not using the term "Providence," most Deists referred to "the Creator" or the "Author of Our Being."

No less eloquent than the Declaration, and far more original, was a document that Jefferson drafted in the following year. Though he composed the Virginia Statute for Religious Freedom in 1777, it was not enacted by the legislature until 1786, and then only with the adroit aid of James Madison while the author was serving as U.S. Minister in Paris. That its adoption was not even later is remarkable. It was the product of a sophisticated mind in a sophisticated society. It was the first statute in the history of the world to declare that there was no religious view whose expression should in any way "diminish, enlarge, or affect" the "civil capacities" of the speaker or writer.

With consummate skill, Jefferson turned the tables on those who would charge him with impiety. In the preamble, he condemned "the legislators and rulers, civil as well as ecclesiastical, who, being themselves but fallible and uninspired men, have assumed impious presumption of dominion over the faith of others." Subsequent phrases asserted that "Almighty God hath created the mind free, that all attempts to influence it by temporal punishments or burthens or by civil incapacitations, tend only to beget habits of hypocrisy and meanness, and are a departure from the plan of the Holy Author of our religion, who, being Lord both of body and mind, yet chose not to propagate it by coercions on either, as was in his Almighty power to do."

Other portions of the statute were phrased with a bold originality to match the spirit of the legislation. "Our civil rights," Jefferson wrote, "have no dependence on our religious opinions, more than on our opinions in physics and geometry. . . . The legitimate powers of government extend only to such acts as are injurious to others. But it does me no injury for my neighbor to say there are twenty gods or no god. It neither picks my pocket nor breaks my leg."

Jefferson anticipated the argument that a nonbeliever should at least be restrained from propagating errors. He wrote into the statute, "Constraint may make him worse by making him a hypocrite, but it will never make him a truer man." He declared his conviction "that truth is great and will prevail if left to herself, that she is the proper and sufficient antagonist to error, and has nothing to fear from the conflict, unless by human interposition disarmed of her natural weapons, free argument and debate, errors ceasing to be dangerous when it is permitted freely to contradict them."

The sweeping character of the statute is specifically delineated: "*Be it therefore enacted by the General Assembly,* that no man shall be compelled to frequent or support any religious worship, place or ministry whatsoever, nor shall be enforced, restrained, molested, or burthened in his body or goods, nor shall otherwise suffer on account of his religious opinions or belief, but that all men shall be free to profess, and by argument to maintain, their opinions in matters of religion, and that the same shall in no wise diminish, enlarge, or affect their civil capacities."

So much for a declaration in the dispassionate language of the law. In the next few lines, Jefferson cast off the theoretical detachment of the drafter of legislation and abandoned the supposed disinterestedness of the Enlightenment scholar. His emotions were so deeply involved that this skilled parliamentarian consciously departed from parliamentary practice. He wrote into the statute itself, "Though we well know that . . . to declare this act irrevocable would be of no effect in law, yet we are free to declare that if any act shall be hereafter passed to repeal the present, or to narrow rights hereby asserted . . . such act will be an infringement of natural right."

Jefferson's passionate concern for religious freedom cannot be doubted. The emotional addendum to the statute makes that entirely clear. But the statute tells us nothing of his personal religious convictions. They had no place in an act of the legislature. Jefferson's emotions did not betray him into forgetfulness on that point. Besides, this man who often spoke unguardedly on many matters was extremely reticent on the subject of his faith.

His public utterances therefore furnish few clues to his personal religious convictions. But there are some. As a candidate for president in 1801, he disdained to answer the charge that he was an atheist, but in his first inaugural address he said the American people were "enlightened by a benign religion, professed, indeed, and practiced in various forms, yet all of them inculcating honesty, truth, temperance, gratitude, and the love of man; acknowledging and adoring an overruling Providence, which by all its dispensations proves that it delights in the happiness of man here and his greater happiness hereafter."

Some may say that Jefferson, like some other politicians, may have expressed a religious sentiment just to win public approval. But would a man who, as a vote-seeking candidate, scorned to repudiate the charge of atheism have stooped as victor to false pretenses about his religion? We can accept at face value Jefferson's intimation of faith in a benevolent God.

Four years later, at his second inauguration, Jefferson said that he would need a continuation of the "indulgence" he had "heretofore experienced." He added, "I shall need, too, favor of that Being in whose hands we are, who led our forefathers, as Israel of old, from their native land and planted them in a country flowing with all the necessaries and comforts of life, who has covered our infancy with His providence and our riper years with His wisdom and power, and to whose goodness I ask you to join with me in supplications that He will so enlighten the minds of your servants, guide their councils and prosper their measures, that whatsoever they do shall result in your good, and shall secure to you the peace, friendship, and approbation of all nations."

These words seemed to go beyond the religious statement of the First Inaugural in that they appeared to reflect faith in the efficacy of prayer and a rewarding afterlife.

A word master, Jefferson chose his words with special care in what was a message to posterity as well as to his fellow citizens. In using the phrase "*enlightened* by a benign religion," he refuted the contention that his philosophy held enlightenment and religion to be irreconcilable enemies.

Some reassured by this statement were disturbed again when he refused to proclaim days of prayer or religious thanksgiving. To do so, he said, would be to violate the separation of church and state. The attitude of President Jefferson on this question was quite different from that of Jefferson the young legislator.

Our most reliable and precise information on Jefferson's religious views is in his private writings to the few friends to whom he confided them. One of his chief confidants was John Adams in the years when both had retired from political office. They had worked shoulder to shoulder in the Revolutionary councils of the new nation. Adams had nominated Jefferson to be the chief author of the Declaration of Independence. But when patriots split into political parties, Adams was the Federalist president and Jefferson was the leader of the Republican opposition. The friendship did not survive the contest, but it was resurrected in the years when they withdrew from active combat.

To Adams on July 5, 1814, Jefferson wrote, "The doctrines that flowed from the lips of Jesus himself are within the comprehension of a child; but thousands of volumes have not yet explained the Platonisms engrafted on them, and for this obvious reason, that nonsense can never be explained."

Plato is generally honored as one of the greatest geniuses in the story of civilization. Alfred North Whitehead, one of the most brilliant of twentieth-century mathematicians and philosophers, called Plato the outstanding mind in human history. But Jefferson felt an almost personal antipathy for the great Greek and blamed him for introducing needless mystification into both philosophy and theology. He blamed St. Paul for muddying with cloudy Platonisms the pure springs of Jesus' thought.

Jefferson rejected the trinitarian concept of Father, Son, and Holy Ghost (Spirit). Once he wrote to Adams, "It is too late in the day for men of sincerity to pretend they believe in the Platonic mysticisms that three are one, and one is three; and yet that the one is not three, and the three are not one. . . . But this constitutes the craft, the power, and the profit of the priests."

For much of his life, Jefferson referred to ministers of every denomination as priests. For him, the term was pejorative. He repeatedly linked priests and kings as enemies of individual freedom who used superstition as an instrument of tyranny. He wrote to Adams, "We should all then, like the Quakers, live without an order of priests, moralize for ourselves, follow the oracle of conscience, and say nothing about what no man can understand, nor therefore believe."

"The Christian priesthood," he said, "finding the doctrines of Christ leveled to every understanding, and too plain to need explanation, saw in the mysticism of Plato materials with which they might build up an artificial system which might, from its indistinctness, admit everlasting controversy, give employment for their order, and introduce it to power, profit, and pre-eminence."

Because he believed that the clergy exercised undue power through collaboration with agents of the state, he believed that they should automatically be barred from political office. He went so far as to call them "the real Anti-Christ."

He told Baron von Humboldt, "History, I believe, furnishes no example of a priest-ridden people maintaining a free civil government." In public utterances, he called for a wall of separation between church and state. Privately, he referred to "this loathsome combination of church and state."

The image of a wall between church and state has been cited frequently since. In 1947, in *Emerson v. Board of Education*, U.S. Supreme Court Justice Hugo LaFayette Black declared, "The first Amendment has erected a wall between church and state. That wall must be kept high and impregnable. We could not approve the slightest breach." As the twentieth century drew to a close, the image was being cited more often than at any previous time in American history. People differed widely on the stringency of the separation that Jefferson had called for.

Significantly, Daniel L. Dreisbach points out in *Thomas Jefferson and the Wall of Separation between Church and State* (p. 22) that Jefferson "frequently attended . . . religious services in the [nation's] capitol." In a letter to Thomas Cooper, Jefferson boasted of the harmonious arrangement among four denominations that permitted them to hold services in the Charlottesville courthouse on successive Sundays.

Fortunately, it is not necessary to define Jefferson's religious views solely in terms of his hostilities. He has left an enduring written record that testifies directly to positive elements of his faith. No less impressive is the implicit concern that inspired such a labor of love. Though augmented by a few letters to trusted friends, the written record consists primarily of two compilations, the first of which Jefferson began amid the manifold duties of a busy presidency whose accomplishments have seldom been equaled. This first volume was *The Philosophy of Jesus*. The second was *The Life and*

Morals of Jesus. Since Jefferson's death, the two have been published both together and in separate covers in various editions.

The two works mark the distance that Jefferson had traveled in a journey of faith since his first intensive study of Bolingbroke and Kames when he was a young man. He had then copied into his "Literary Bible" or "Commonplace Book" many more quotations from the Epicurean and Stoic philosophers than from Jesus or any other Biblical source. He had accepted Bolingbroke's judgment that a "system of ethics . . . collected from writings of ancient heathen moralists, of Tully, of Seneca, of Epictetus, and others, would be more full, more entire, more coherent and more clearly deduced from unquestionable principles of knowledge" than any sayings attributed to Jesus."

By the time Jefferson completed his two Jesus-centered compilations, he concluded that the Nazarene's precepts were "the most pure, benevolent, and sublime which have ever been preached to man."

Jefferson's terms of reference to the Deity over the length of his career suggest an increasing intimacy. In the Declaration of Independence, "Creator" was the favored term. His usage of "God," supported by a qualifying adjective, emerged as a reminder of the "natural law" so dear to Enlightenment scientists and philosophers. "Nature's God" lacked the personal quality of "my God" or "our God" or even the freestanding "God." But it was acceptable to trendy intellectuals, even some in Paris. Sometimes, ironically echoing Plato, whom he intensely disliked, he referred to the "Great First Cause." But in later years he talked about a "merciful Providence," conferring personality on an abstraction. Long before his death, he was counseling youngsters in his family to "adore God."

Atheists, he wrote to John Adams on April 8, 1816, "composed a numerous school in the Catholic countries while the infidelity of the Protestant took generally the form of Theism. The former always insisted that it was a mere question of definition between them, the hypostasis of which on both sides was 'Nature' or 'the

Universe': that both agreed in the order of the existing system, but the one supposed it from eternity, the other as having begun in time."

"And when the atheist," Jefferson said, "descanted on the unceasing motion and circulation of matter through the animal, vegetable and mineral kingdoms, never resting, never annihilated, always changing form, and under all forms gifted with the power of reproduction, the Theist pointing 'to the heavens above, and to the earth beneath, and to the waters under the earth,' asked if these did not proclaim a first cause, possessing intelligence and power; power in the production, and intelligence in the design and constant preservation of the system; urged the palpable existence of final causes, that the eye was made to see, and the ear to hear, and not that we see because we have eyes, and hear because we have ears."

The mature Jefferson's sympathies as between atheists and theists are quite clear. Like the Psalmist of old, he proclaims that "the heavens declare the glory of God." The "argument from design" not only is common in folk speculation but also has been enunciated by philosophers ranging from Socrates and Xenophon to William Paley and was even adjusted to the concept of Darwinian evolution by twentieth-century giant Henri Bergson.

Before Jefferson was seventy-four years old, the Deity was no longer an embodiment of pure justice but rather a spirit of love. On January 11, 1817, the Virginian wrote Abigail Adams, "That God is an essentially benevolent Being is shown by His goodness in stealing away our faculties of enjoyment one by one, searing our sensibilities, until, satiated and fatigued by this ceaseless iteration, we ask our own congé."

Jefferson's repeated criticisms of "priest-ridden" societies and his assertion that history revealed to him no example of political freedom surviving in such a society caused many people to conclude that he was hostile to all ministers. Such was not the case. One of his dearest friends was Joseph Priestley, a liberal clergyman as well as a distinguished scientist. Other ministers won his respect and friendship. One of these was a Baptist minister, Rev. Mr. Hiter, an itinerant, circuit-riding preacher. In his last years, Jefferson often attended services conducted by Mr. Hiter. Once, when the former president was riding his horse back to Monticello after supervising construction on the grounds of the University of Virginia, he came upon an outdoor service addressed by this favorite clergyman. Though Jefferson was wearing overalls, he hesitated only a moment before joining the congregation. In the meeting, a collection was made to buy the preacher a new horse. Jefferson promptly rose from his seat, pulled a handful of coins from his pocket, and thrust them into the clergyman's hands.

Jefferson credited various ministers with works beneficial to society, but he was distrustful of alliances between church and state. An established church was anathema to him.

He was largely free of denominational prejudices, though he resented "New England divines" who warned that he was the anti-Christ. Students of his life disagree as to whether he was an Episcopal vestryman, but he was at least nominally an Episcopalian. He was christened in an Anglican ceremony and married by an Anglican priest. An Episcopal clergyman presided at his funeral rites. Whether or not he was a vestryman has little bearing on his personal religious views in a society where vestries had political as well as religious responsibilities and their members' creedal allegiances were less important than their patriotism.

Though Jefferson deplored the political activities of the Catholic Church and did not want his daughters to become members, he sent one of them to a parochial school when he was living in Paris. His broad tolerance of the Protestant denominations was indicated by his praise of the Quakers and his delight in the fact that a Charlottesville sanctuary was shared by Episcopalians, Presbyterians, Methodists, and Baptists. His tolerance of various forms of worship was not limited to Christians. Though he saw Christ as the reformer of a desensitized Jewish faith, he spoke admiringly of Jews in his own time.

The year 1776 was for Jefferson a threefold year of independence, one in which he publicly declared an end to his country's colonial status and advocated religious freedom while confiding to friends his conviction that the true principles of Jesus were to be found in the gospels rather than the epistles. Jefferson did not accept as literal truth everything in the gospels. He apparently believed that they were inspired by God, but he did not believe that every word was dictated by Him. He believed that they were composed by fallible men who, however conscientious they might be, were subject to the usual limitations of human knowledge and intelligence. In fact, he noted that they were not even among the best educated people of their time and place. But in general, he trusted their reporting of the words of Jesus. These he included in his own quadrilingual version of the New Testament.

For distortion of Christ's teachings, Jefferson blamed not the simple fishermen among the apostles but rather a sophisticated, well-educated product of Greek, Roman, and Jewish cultures. Saul of Tarsus, who saw the light on the road to Damascus and became Saint Paul, was to Jefferson the archvillain in the history of Christianity. Jefferson saw Plato as the great distorter of Western philosophy, and he viewed Paul as a Platonist who had brought beclouding mysticism to Jesus' clear moral teachings. Jefferson included Matthew, Mark, Luke, and John's quotations from Jesus in his versions of the New Testament, carefully excluding all references to miracles, saying that there was no historical evidence to prove that they were not the products of superstition or overheated imaginations. The epistles of Paul he excluded altogether. He said that he had no difficulty separating the treasure from the "dung."

Jefferson's *Philosophy of Jesus* and his *Life and Morals of Jesus* are often confused with each other, even by well-educated persons for whom the Virginian is a favorite hero. Sometimes the mistake has been made by professional scholars. Some people have assumed that the titles are two different names for the same book.

The Life and Morals of Jesus consists of selected verses from the New Testament placed in parallel columns of Greek, Latin, French, and the English of the King James version. Jefferson's immediate family and some of his intimate friends were fully aware of his compilation's existence. Three years after his death, the general public learned of it from the publication of a memoir by the President's grandson.

But *The Philosophy of Jesus*, consisting entirely of selections from the English Bible's books of Matthew, Mark, Luke, and John, remained unknown to his children and grandchildren. Without the evidence of letters that Jefferson wrote to some of his closest friends, especially Joseph Priestley, John Adams, and Benjamin Rush, a casual reader of the book might not suspect that the scholarly statesman had systematically eliminated all references to miracles and the supernatural. Jefferson did not advertise his rejection of the mystical accounts in the Bible. Most readers probably would take at face value his title-page description of the work as an "abridgement of the New Testament for the use of the Indians unembarrassed with matters of faith beyond the level of their comprehension."

He once outlined a comparison of Jesus' teachings with those of such classical philosophers as Pythagoras, Socrates, Epicurus, Epictetus, Seneca, and Antoninus and seriously contemplated writing a book on the subject, but never did.

What did Jefferson think about religion? The question invites another: At what age? Glib answers to questions about anyone's views on complex matters are meaningless or misleading when no time is specified. Such questions make no allowance for the evolution of thought characteristic of most people, especially those with expanding intellects. Henry Adams wrote that Jefferson, alone among all the early presidents, "could be painted only touch by touch, with a fine pencil, and the perfection of the likeness depended upon the shifting and uncertain flicker of the transparent shadows." Ever since, too much has been written about the paradoxical thoughts of the third president. Often the charge of self-contradiction falls short of the target, unless the opinions of the youthful Tom Jefferson are presented side by side with those of the young legislator, the president in his prime, and the aged Sage of Monticello. It is unreasonable that Jefferson, through a process of rhetorical reincarnation, should be made to debate with himself.

When Jefferson the college student abandoned his teenaged agnosticism, he still insisted that the admonitions of the Stoic philosophers constituted a code of ethics superior to that advocated by Jesus. Jefferson seemed to be on the verge of embracing Epictetus with all the fervor of Conrad Hensley in Tom Wolfe's *A Man in Full*. A little later he regarded the Stoic and Christian codes as of equal value.

As President, on April 3, 1803, he mailed to Benjamin Rush a syllabus in which he said of Jesus:

> His moral doctrines relating to kindred and friends were more pure and perfect than those of the most correct of the philosophers, and greatly more so than those of the Jews. And they went far beyond both in inculcating universal philanthropy, not only to kindred and friends, to neighbors and countrymen, gathering all into one family, under the bonds of love, charity, peace, common wants, and common aids. A development of this head will evince the peculiar superiority of the system of Jesus over all others.

Jefferson added, "The precepts of philosophy, and of the Hebrew code, laid hold of actions only. He pushed his scrutinies into the heart of man, erected his tribunal in the region of his thoughts and purified the waters at the fountain head."

Jefferson's next statement prompts further speculation about his views at the time. He says of Jesus, "He taught, emphatically, the doctrine of a future state; which was either doubted or disbelieved by the Jews: and wielded it with efficacy, as an important incentive, supplementary to the other motives to moral conduct."

Did Jefferson, when he wrote these words, believe in the doctrines of an afterlife, or did he simply believe it to have been a useful tool in the propagation of Christian faith? Perhaps, at this stage, he had no real conviction on the point.

By October 12, 1813, he had broadened his appreciation of the

Bible beyond the New Testament to include the Psalms. In replying to John Adams, who seemed to suggest that the hymn of Cleanthes to Jupiter was equal, if not superior, to the Psalms, Jefferson wrote:

I acknowledge all the merit of the hymn of Cleanthes to Jupiter which you ascribe to it. It is as highly sublime as a chaste and correct imagination can permit itself to go. Yet in the contemplation of a being so superlative, the hyperbolic flights of the Psalmist may often be followed with approbation, even with rapture; and I have no hesitation in giving him the palm over all the hymnists of every language and of every time. Turn to the 148th psalm. . . . Have such conceptions been ever before expressed?

Jefferson continued to balk at the concept of virgin birth. On April 11, 1823, he wrote to Adams,

The truth is that the greatest enemies of the doctrines of Jesus are those calling themselves the expositors of them, who have perverted them for the structure of a system of fancy absolutely incomprehensible, and without any foundation in his genuine words. And the day will come when the mystical generation of Jesus by the supreme being as his father in the womb of a virgin will be classed with the fable of the generation of Minerva in the brain of Jupiter. But we may hope that the dawn of reason and freedom of thought in these United States will do away [with] all this artificial scaffolding, and restore to us the primitive and genuine doctrines of this the most venerated reformer of human errors.

In this same letter, however, Jefferson espoused the traditional Christian view of eternal life. He said that, like Adams, in contemplating death, he was content to submit to the will of "the God of Jesus, and our God." He concluded the message to his old friend, "I join you cordially, and await his time and will with more readiness than reluctance. May we meet there again [in the next world], in

Congress, with our ancient colleagues, and receive with them the seal of approbation 'well done, good and faithful servants.'"

Some of Jefferson's conventional words at his first inauguration as president had suggested a belief in eternal life. In his last years, he anticipated the joys of reuniting with loved ones after death. But much earlier, in 1782, he had had inscribed on the tombstone of his beloved wife Patty not a Christian quotation but the less hopeful words of Achilles to Patroclus over Hector's corpse in the twenty-second book of the *Iliad*: "If in the next world men forget their dead, yet will I even there remember my dead companion."

His prejudice against the clergy yielded to affectionate respect and eventually fast friendship for such men of the cloth as Joseph Priestley, Ezra Stiles, Jared Sparks, and the Rev. Mr. Hite. He was largely free of denominational hostilities, though he had bitter memories of the terms in which some Congregational ministers in New England had denounced him from their pulpits. He expressed sympathy for Jews and Quakers who were victims of discrimination. As Minister to Paris, he had given one of his daughters the advantage of a good Catholic school even though he did not want her to become a Catholic. He often regarded the league between Catholic Church and royal government as the most conspicuous example of unholy alliance between church and state, but with the passage of years he became more appreciative of the good works of individual Catholics, perhaps particularly after his beloved Maria Cosway became the head of a Catholic school.

On February 21, 1825, a little more than a year before his death, Jefferson wrote to his namesake, Thomas Jefferson Smith, a letter to be read when the little boy had matured enough to understand it. In part, it said, "Adore God . . . Love your neighbors as yourself, and your country more than yourself. Be just. Be true. Murmur not at the ways of Providence. So shall the life into which you have entered be the portal to one of eternal and ineffable bliss. And if to the dead it is permitted to care for the things of this world, every action of your life will be under my regard."

As late as 1830, the Philadelphia Public Library refused to place books about Jefferson on its shelves. It did so because of the belief that he was an atheist. The irony of this policy in the city that first heard his Declaration of Independence requires no comment. Not only was the prohibition wrong; so was the premise on which it was based. If Jefferson had ever been a youthful atheist, he had soon moved on to agnosticism, then to a faith grounded in classical and Biblical sources, and finally to an unorthodox Christianity.

Through all the changes in the evolution of Jefferson's faith, there was at least one point of consistency, a devotion to the ideal of religious liberty. A quotation from John Locke that he invoked at least once would have expressed his views at any stage of adulthood: "The care of every man's soul belongs to himself." Fittingly, in composing the inscription for his tombstone, he listed with the authorship of the Declaration of Independence and the founding of the University of Virginia a third major accomplishment: the writing of the Virginia Statute for Religious Freedom.

How did his religious opinions affect his public career? Doubtless in many undocumented ways. But also in some for which there is abundant evidence. His opposition to slavery manifested in his repeated efforts to eliminate both the importation of slaves and slavery itself in his native state, to censure the institution in the Declaration of Independence, and to arrest its spread into future states—all of these were driven by a passion beyond the cool dictates of Enlightenment philosophy. They find expression in his anguished cry: "Can the liberties of a nation be thought secure when we have removed their only firm basis, a conviction in the minds of the people that these liberties are of the gift of God? That they are not to be violated but with his wrath? Indeed, I tremble for my country when I reflect that God is just, that his justice cannot sleep forever. . . . Amen."

Jefferson's faith shines through, too, in the words of his Virginia Statute for Religious Freedom, one of a handful of noblest public documents in the history of the world.

3

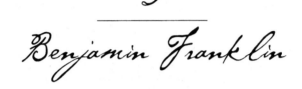

Benjamin Franklin

WHEN Thomas Jefferson, in his famous *Notes on the State of Virginia*, wrote, "it does me no injury for my neighbor to say there are twenty gods or no god," he was stating two extreme positions summoned by his imagination. A colleague of his in the committee charged with preparing a Declaration of Independence, and in continental diplomacy, had at different times in his career advanced both propositions. The man was Benjamin Franklin.

That Franklin should have been an adolescent atheist is not surprising. Many precocious youngsters pass through a stage of atheism, sometimes on the way to a satisfying faith. But many people will be surprised to learn that Franklin at age twenty-two, after much reading of scientific literature and conversations with London savants, solemnly declared his belief in a plurality of gods.

Franklin was so serious in his polytheism that he composed a creed, headed "First Principles," which he called his "little liturgy." It was the central constituent of his "Articles of Belief and Acts of Religion." He sounds like a monotheist when his creed begins with the words: "I believe there is one Supreme most perfect Being." But the implications change radically when that Being is identified in the same sentence as "Author and Father of the Gods themselves."

In words that seem an anticipation of space-age science fiction, Franklin says,

When I stretch my imagination through and beyond our system of planets, beyond the visible fixed stars themselves, into that space that is every way infinite, and conceive it filled with suns like ours, each with a chorus of worlds forever moving round him, then this little ball on which we move seems, even in my narrow imagination, to be almost nothing, and myself less than nothing, and of no sort of consequence.

Franklin then envisions a Supreme Being very different from the Christian God whose "eye is on the sparrow." He says,

I imagine it great vanity in me to suppose that the *Supremely Perfect* does in the least regard such an inconsiderable nothing as man. More especially, since it is impossible for me to have any positive clear idea of that which is infinite and incomprehensible. I cannot conceive otherwise than that He, *the Infinite Father*, expects or requires no worship or praise from us, but that he is even INFINITELY ABOVE IT.

Nevertheless, Franklin believed that "there is in all men something like a natural principle which inclines them to devotion or the worship of some unseen power." He concludes, "I think it seems required of me, and my duty, as a man, to pay divine regards to something."

Here he introduces a startling idea:

I conceive then that the Infinite has created many Beings or Gods, vastly superior to Men, who can better conceive his perfections than we, and return him a more rational and glorious praise. As among men the praise of the ignorant or of children is not regarded by the ingenious painter or architect, who is rather honored and pleased with the approbation of wise men and artists.

It may be that these created Gods are immortal, or it may be that, after many ages, they are changed, and others supply their places.

Howbeit, I conceive that each of these is exceedingly wise, and good, and very powerful; and that each has made for himself one glorious sun, attended with a beautiful and admirable system of planets.

It is that particular wise and good God who is the Author and Owner of our system that I propose for the object of my praise and admiration.

Franklin conceived that this "Owner" of our solar system, unlike the Infinite Father "infinitely above" a need for the praise of ignorant man, "has in himself some of those passions he has planted in us, and that, since he has given us Reason whereby we are capable of observing his wisdom in the Creation, he is not above caring for us, being pleased with our praise, and offended when we slight him or neglect his glory."

Saying that he would "be happy to have so wise, good, and powerful a Being my friend," Franklin considered "in what manner I shall make myself most acceptable to him." He concluded, "Next to the praise resulting from his wisdom, I believe he is pleased and delights in the happiness of those he has created; and since without virtue man can have no happiness in this world, firmly believe he delights to see me virtuous, because he is pleased when he sees me happy."

THE CONCEPT of a Supreme Being presiding over a congeries of solar systems was revolutionary. But there was nothing revolutionary to Christian ears in an admonition to people to worship their benevolent Creator, who was also the Creator of the solar system, and to please Him and simultaneously make themselves happy by leading virtuous lives. Of course, there was room for differences of opinion over what constituted virtue. Franklin said, "And since he has created many things which seem purely designed for the delight of man, I believe he is not offended when he sees his children solace themselves in any manner of pleasant exercises and innocent delights, and I think no pleasure innocent that is to man hurtful." Much would hinge on the definition of "hurtful," and there was no reference to heaven or hell or eternal life. On the surface, though, there was nothing in this creed of Franklin's that prescribed conduct different from that which faithful priests and parsons throughout Christendom recommended to their flocks.

The chief radical element in Franklin's thought was the supposition that the God who had created our solar system was subordinate to a still greater Deity. The concept of coexistent gods of differing powers was common to many primitive tribes and had even existed in Israel, Greece, and Rome in periods of considerable cultural achievements. Milton, in *Paradise Lost*, had utilized his audience's vestigial feel for such hierarchical deity when, blurring the distinction between angels and gods, he had Belial and Beelzebub support Satan in rebellion against the God of all. Nevertheless, the concept of the ruler of our solar system as the creation and servant of a greater God was a strange one indeed to be advanced by an eighteenth-century Anglo-American intellectual. Contemporary theologians discussed the possibility of inhabited worlds other than Earth but envisioned them all as the work of the same Creator.

What in Franklin's environment nurtured such boldness? He was born in Boston, Massachusetts, in 1706. Though the city's name would later become linked historically with revolutionary activity, it was then still a bastion of conservatism. Massachusetts was in fact, if not officially, a theocracy. At home in England and during their self-imposed exile in Holland, the Puritans had been rebels. But in Massachusetts they had built their own society, which they were confident was ordained by God. And like so many others who have suffered persecution, they had then begun to persecute people whose mores and beliefs differed from their own.

But some of Franklin's family had been rebels in Massachusetts. His maternal grandfather, Peter Folger of Nantucket, was the author of *A Looking-Glass for the Times*, a work that attacked the persecutors of Quakers and Baptists. Benjamin's father, Josiah Franklin, was a Congregationalist, a member of the sect that dominated Massachusetts, but he was a rebel himself in embracing that faith, the Franklins having been Anglicans ever since the founding of the established church in the reign of Henry VIII. There was boldness in Josiah's embarking for America, leaving forever the thirty-acre farm in Ecton Parish on which his family had lived and worked for three centuries.

Nevertheless, young Benjamin's home life was strictly in accord with the dictates of the Massachusetts theocracy. He learned to read so early in life and so quickly that he could not remember acquiring the skill, and by age five he was reading the Bible. He read *Pilgrim's Progress* and various volumes of religious inspiration and conservative theology.

Impressed with the boy's precocious interest in religious texts, a paternal uncle wrote, "If the buds are so precious, what may we expect when the fruit is ripe?" Benjamin was Josiah's tenth child, and the father began to think of him as his tithe to the church. He wanted to have him educated for the ministry. In Massachusetts, where Congregational ministers dominated society, Benjamin might some day speak with authority on the many religious issues that his polemical father debated so fervently with anyone who would listen. Meanwhile, Josiah lectured the boy so strenuously on the "Eternal Decrees of God" and the doctrines of election and reprobation that even such a brilliant youngster became utterly confused.

Some of Benjamin's readings were in books that made him conscious of the individual's obligation to serve society as well as to avoid evil. One was Cotton Mather's *Essays to Do Good*, by a member of one of the clerical clans dominating education as well as worship in Massachusetts. But another was Daniel Defoe's *Essay on Projects*, which considered social responsibility in secular as well as religious terms. Another favorite book of his was Plutarch's *Lives*. Its delineation of the characters of great Greeks and Romans was a reminder that virtuous careers had been pursued by some who had not known the blessings of either Judaism or Christianity.

When Benjamin's father realized that he lacked the money to educate the youngster for the ministry, the boy concluded that he would not have a college education. But by that time his intellectual curiosity was so aroused that he was determined to educate himself by wide reading.

Apprenticed to his older brother James, a Boston printer and newspaper publisher, he had access to publications that aroused his interest in a variety of subjects. Unlike almost all other newspapermen in Massachusetts, James dared to print criticisms of both Congregational clergymen and public officials. Some of his paper's cleverest articles were anonymously written by one whose identity was unknown even to him. Apparently he never discovered his brother Benjamin slipping these articles under the door.

When James's editorial criticism of Massachusetts officials earned him a month in jail, sixteen-year-old Benjamin edited the paper. When the two brothers quarreled subsequently, the younger walked out nearly two years ahead of the legal expiration of his indenture.

As James circulated word that his brother had deserted him, no other Bostonian would hire him. When a search for employment in New York proved fruitless, Benjamin eventually settled in Philadelphia. Despite his Boston birth, and residence for a while in London, it was with Philadelphia that he would always be identified.

The move from Boston to Philadelphia probably influenced his views on religion and many other subjects. It certainly helped him to attain a position that has made his views on religion and other topics a matter of great interest down to our own time. The Boston environment of his day nurtured a narrow bookishness but discouraged broad scholarship. New England, especially Massachusetts, in those days lagged behind both the Middle Colonies and the South in the advancement of natural science and was decidedly less hospitable to free philosophical speculation. Alfred Owen Aldridge, a distinguished biographer of both Jonathan Edwards and Benjamin Franklin, has said that the great mystery about Edwards is not how a man of his intellect and studious habits failed to become a more complete philosopher but rather "how a philosopher of any eminence at all could have sprung from the provincial intellectual milieu of New England in the first decade of the eighteenth century." He provocatively points out that "Benjamin Franklin, only three years Edwards's junior, whose life presents intriguing parallels and contrasts, rose from essentially the same environment but escaped at an early age to a more cosmopolitan atmosphere."

It is sometimes difficult for Americans of our time to realize that even Harvard University, now internationally famous for deep and bold studies in many fields, was once an intellectually restricted bastion of conformity. Philadelphia was, in contrast to Boston, soon the second largest metropolis in the English-speaking world and a stimulating intersection of intellect and commerce. Founded by William Penn, England's most famous Quaker, Pennsylvania was a Quaker province and Philadelphia was the Quaker City; but their inhabitants enjoyed such religious freedom as New Englanders had known only in Roger Williams's Rhode Island and for gleaming intervals in parts of Connecticut.

In addition to the adherents of a variety of Christian sects attracted by Pennsylvania's religious tolerance, Philadelphia was attracting adherents of a secular faith embraced with fervor by many intellectuals in Europe and America. That was the Enlightenment.

Too many people today think of the Enlightenment as a godless philosophy chiefly French in origin and practice. Some who claimed the Enlightenment label were atheists, but they were exceeded in number by those who asserted that human reason was a gift from God to be used to solve all human problems. And far from being merely a French contagion spread to Americans by the careless handling of books from Paris, it was apparently a spontaneous growth indigenous to a dozen or more Western nations. France had its Voltaire, Rousseau, Diderot, Turgot, and Condorcet. But the German states had their Leibnitz, Lessing, and Herder, and Britain had its Locke, Hume, Smith, and Priestley. And America would have its Jefferson and Franklin. Far from being mere imitations of European models, these last two men were of sufficient stature to evoke from Crane Brinton, writing on the Enlightenment for the eight-volume *Encyclopedia of Philosophy*, the judgment that "we could do much worse" than cite them as representatives of the whole international movement.

Some of these philosophes stopped reading any version of the Holy Bible, though others, such as Jefferson and Priestley, became earnest students of it. All, however, from whatever land, were assiduous readers of the "Book of Nature." All believed themselves to be devotees of Reason, and they studied this primary text.

Most believed that, by applying reason in reading the "Book of Nature," humanity could eventually attain perfection. As a young man, Franklin believed that perfection was a reasonable goal not only for society but also for individual lives. He deemed the cultivation of thirteen particular virtues to be necessary to this achievement. These included moderation, tranquility, humility, temperance, silence, order, resolution, sincerity, justice, and cleanliness. Another was frugality, a quality for which Franklin's name is synonymous to most Americans. The struggle for one virtue, chastity, gave him a great deal of trouble. He characterized the sexual drive as "that hard-to-be-governed Passion of Youth" but belied the restrictions of the reference by the richly erotic imagery of his writings as a white-haired elder statesman. In the category "humility," he placed the admonition, "Imitate Jesus and Socrates." He was not renouncing the founder of Christianity, but he did seem to place the ancient Greek philosopher on the same plane.

He assigned each virtue its own page in a little notebook. For each day of the week there was a space for the recording of self-assigned demerits. Franklin resolved to count the battle for virtue won when his honestly kept record showed no infractions for a period of thirteen weeks. Meanwhile, when the pages were filled, he would erase the record of violations and start over anew. Eventually, erasures filled the pages with holes. When Franklin was a world figure, he still used his little notebook, but he had substituted durable sheets of ivory for the fragile paper pages.

The list of virtues might serve the ethical purposes of an atheist or agnostic as readily as those of a believer. But the epigraph that he affixed to his calendar of virtues indicated that, however unorthodox he might be, he was nevertheless a believer. The addition was the same that he had made to his litany, "Articles of Belief." It was a quotation from Joseph Addison's *Cato*: "Here will I hold—If there is a Pow'r above us (And that there is, all Nature cries aloud Thro' all her Works), He must delight in Virtue And that which he delights in must be Happy."

Addison was coeditor of *The Spectator* with his friend Sir Richard Steele, and the resulting volumes of *Spectator* essays became enduring classics of English literature. Franklin admired them as much for their style as their substance, quoted them frequently, and consciously modeled his own literary expression upon theirs. By this time, he had modeled his mode of discourse upon the practice of Socrates, substituting skilled questioning for the argumentative habits that had sometimes irritated his associates.

He was still affected by an essay that he had read in his early teens and that had profoundly influenced his religious attitudes. This was an attempted refutation of Deism by one who favored the concept of a personal God. Franklin found the Deist statements against which the author argued more convincing than the writer's own arguments. But he did not embrace either atheism or agnosticism. At age twenty-two, in a clever epitaph that he composed for himself, Franklin expressed both faith in a benevolent God and belief in the immortality of the soul:

> The body of Benjamin Franklin, Printer (like the cover of an old book; its contents torn out and stripped of its lettering and gilding), lies here, food for worms; but the work shall not be lost, for it will (as he believed) appear once more in a new and more elegant edition, revised and corrected by the Author.

From his twenties into his eighties, Franklin repeatedly emphasized a link between virtue and happiness, sometimes inverting the advice "be good and you will be happy," transforming it into "be happy and you will be good." He frequently said that virtue could lead to happiness, but cited its rewards in material terms. In Part II of his *Autobiography*, Franklin notes, "Nothing so likely to make a man's fortune as virtue." He says in the same book that he had become convinced that "no qualities were so likely to make a poor man's fortune as those of probity and integrity." He often advised young men that these attributes would make them invaluable to "rich merchants, nobility, states, and princes who have need of honest instruments for the management of their affairs." In his *Poor Richard's Almanac* in 1735 he wrote one of the most famous sayings in the English language: "Early to bed and early to rise, makes a man healthy, wealthy, and wise." Apparently virtue was not its own reward. Even health and wisdom were not enough unless joined in a triumvirate with wealth. The implied moral is more reminiscent of Horatio Alger than of John Bunyan.

When quite young, and nowhere near as learned in philosophy as he became, Franklin sometimes used the words "Deist" and "atheist" interchangeably. He later learned to distinguish the two. No one can be simultaneously a Deist and an atheist. The words "Deism" and "Deist" are derived from "Deus," Latin for God.

Deism is a concept of God, and as such cannot represent the view of one who believes there is no God. Within the ranks of Deists, there are many subtle variations in belief, but for each individual these cluster around one or both of two poles. One of these is the belief that God can be known only through the use of reason in examining nature. The other is the belief that God created the universe but since creation has not intervened in its operation.

Though Franklin, after initial confusion, learned the difference between Deism and atheism, many of his contemporaries did not, and most people in successive generations, when they have thought about the matter at all, have assumed that "Deist" and "atheist" are alternate designations for a godless person. It is chiefly because of this confusion that some people have glibly assumed that Franklin had no religion at all.

Historians usually have surmised that Franklin almost certainly adhered to the Deist school of thought that God can be known only through the use of reason in studying the physical universe. They also have concluded that Franklin probably believed that God, having created the universe and set it in motion, had not since interfered in its operation.

Of course, Franklin's idea of a universe whose Creator does not intervene in subsequent events is complicated by his ideas about subordinate gods serving separate worlds. Though he had proposed that the Supreme God remained aloof from human affairs, he had held that the subordinate gods took an active interest in events in their individual worlds. Apparently, Franklin's pantheistic thoughts were not just youthful fancies. Although he says in the *Autobiography* "There is one God, who made all things," this assertion does not rule out the possibility of subordinate deities superintending the operations of worlds created by the great God of all. In 1773, when Franklin was sixty-seven years old, he agreed with a Welsh philosopher that there might be a multiplicity of deities in separate spheres. True, by that time he stated the conception as a possibility rather than an article of faith.

When he was nineteen years old, Franklin produced a pamphlet,

BENJAMIN FRANKLIN

A Dissertation on Liberty and Necessity, Pleasure and Pain, arguing for the existence of a benevolent God but denying the possibility of immortality. He anticipated the criticism that, when wicked people prospered while the good suffered poverty and other misfortune, a benevolent God could provide justice only in a life beyond this world. Franklin's answer was his theory that all people, regardless of external circumstances, experienced in their lives the same amount of pleasure and the same amount of pain. That he should have advanced such an unusual idea before emerging from his teens is not particularly surprising, but that he should have adhered to it for many years is a startling fact. When eventually he abandoned the idea that pleasure and pain were equally distributed among individual human beings, it was not because of the logic that might have been expected of so respected a scientist. He had become so convinced of the wickedness of King George III, regarding him as the foremost international villain of the eighteenth century, that he could not believe that a just God would permit this man to live in luxury unless a harsh fate awaited him in the afterlife. Franklin's reaction was an emotional one produced by his frustration over British policies that threatened American liberties. In reality, George III was not evil incarnate. "Farmer George," as some of his English subjects called him, was a decent family man, who while longing for the life of a cattle farmer, but conscientiously trying to perform regal duties, relied too heavily on the advice of misguided cabinet ministers. Franklin's opinion of George III led him to conclude that "the number and extent of [the King's] crimes" made it impossible that he be justly punished "in this life." The American said that therefore he was "convinced of a future state, in which all that here appears to be wrong shall be set right, all that is crooked made straight."

At various times, Franklin expressed a faith in immortality. On other occasions, his comments on the subject might more accurately be described as expressions of pious hopes. Sometimes he said that it was good that the hope of reward and fear of punishment could be held out to people as an inducement to good behavior. The same observation has been made by many people with strong personal faith in immortality without exciting any suspicion of weasel-wordedness.

Franklin's case, however, is a very special one. He sometimes said that myths could be a powerful support to morals, and he composed some that were accepted as history by many readers. He was also an ardent proponent of the doctrine of social utility as the standard for judging the value of an idea. His approach in society was different from his procedure in the laboratory; in the world of men and women, rather than among his beakers and conductors, he did not ask "Is it true?" so often as he asked "Will the effect be good?"

Another factor to be considered is Franklin's frequent habit of achieving agreement with a correspondent even if he had to confine himself to partial truths, trotting his own views out in costumes more concealing than revealing. He left Boston for Philadelphia in search of greater opportunity, but the range of opportunity in the Massachusetts city was narrowed not only by conditions applicable to the citizenry as a whole but by additional ones in Franklin's own specific case. His argumentative pursuit of religious theories hated by most Bostonians had made him extremely unpopular among his fellow townsmen. He was resolved not to inspire hatred in the future if tactfulness could prevent it.

When Franklin's letters on a particular topic are addressed to people of widely varying views, it is interesting to see how, without telling lies, he often subtly shades his wording to suggest a greater area of agreement with his correspondent than actually exists. As editor and publisher of a newspaper, he sometimes printed hoaxes to enliven his copy. He conscientiously kept the letters to the editor column open to disgruntled readers, but sometimes he pseudonymously wrote letters to the editor lambasting his own editorials. These missives he filled with ignorant errors so that readers of the paper would assume that his opponents were people unqualified to judge.

Franklin's approach to members of various Christian sects was such that John Adams reported, "The Catholics thought him almost a Catholic. The Church of England claimed him as one of them. The Presbyterians thought him half a Presbyterian, and the Friends believed him a wet Quaker." Adams's comment probably contains some truth, even though his statement was colored by his resentment of the Pennsylvanian. When Adams arrived in France to replace one of Franklin's fellow commissioners to its government, he complained that Dr. Franklin's "reputation was more universal than that of Leibnitz or Newton, Frederick or Voltaire. . . . When they spoke of him, they seemed to think he was to restore the Golden Age."

This fame may have increased Franklin's caution in public utterances. He was not just another American public figure. Besides being an elder statesman of his people, he was one of the world's most respected giants of the Enlightenment. He was the inventor of bifocals, the lightning rod, the stove that bore his name, and a new musical instrument, the glass harmonica, for which both Mozart and Beethoven composed. He was a venerated philosopher and one of the world's most widely read writers, frequently quoted in the languages of Continental nations as well as his native English. He was the world's leading scientist in electricity in a time when that field of research was foremost in scholarly and popular concentration.

Small wonder that many clergymen and other defenders of the faith sought his endorsement. Courtesy and a desire for good public relations were probably not the only reasons that Franklin was attentive to their requests. Alfred Owen Aldridge, author of *Benjamin Franklin and Nature's God*, the twentieth century's most thorough student of that subject, wrote, "To him, religion was of primary, not incidental, importance. Franklin found many virtues in religion. To him, discovering the nature of God was the fundamental problem of philosophy."

Franklin's life was filled with triumphs, but also with disappointments. His wife, though a good person and loyal spouse, lacked sufficient education, formal or otherwise, to be a congenial companion to him. His son William, a royal Governor of New Jersey, opposed the cause of American independence for which the father worked so hard and risked so much. Franklin employed his grandson in various tasks, which only revealed the young man's ineptitude. Though Franklin attained the age of eighty-four, an extraordinary milestone in his time, and was honored as America's venerable sage, his last years brought him great physical pain. Through all these trials, he remained most of the time outwardly cheerful and never lost hope for either science or humanity.

In a 1780 letter to Joseph Priestley, distinguished as both scientist and clergyman, Franklin said:

> The rapid progress true science now makes occasions my regret sometimes that I was born too soon. It is impossible to imagine the height to which may be carried, in a thousand years, the power of man over matter. We may perhaps learn to deprive large masses of their gravity, and give them absolute levity for the sake of easy transport. Agriculture may diminish its labor and double its produce; all diseases may by sure means be prevented, or cured, not excepting even that of old age, and our lives lengthened at pleasure even beyond the antediluvian standard. O that moral science were in as fair a way of improvement, that men would cease to be wolves to one another, and that human beings would at length learn what they now improperly call humanity.

Again Aldridge's observations are pertinent. He reminds us, "In his autobiography [Franklin] remarked that 'This is the age of experiments,' and he applied the experimental method to his attempt to unravel the secrets of divinity and morality. No other subject occupied more of his time and reflections."

Franklin believed that making the teachings of Jesus more accessible to the multitudes would accomplish more than any other activity toward the moral reform of humanity. As always, his impulse was not just to talk about a solution but to work personally for one. He exemplified his own philosophy, as expressed in his autobiography and reiterated in letters, that "the most acceptable service of God is doing good to man."

When Franklin learned that an old friend of his, a prominent English nobleman, was eager to collaborate in modernizing the *Book of Common Prayer*, he leaped at the opportunity. Some more discreet reformers might have hesitated because the prospective sponsor was Sir Francis Dashwood, Baron Le Despenser. The baron was famous as an efficient director of England's postal system, but he was also notorious as the presiding officer of the Hellfire Club. At meetings of this organization, some of the ladies wore exquisite masks and nothing else. Franklin was not a member of the club, but was reported to have been its guest at least twice. There is no report of scandalous behavior on his part at any of these sessions, but the combination of his erotic imagination and his insatiable curiosity made the invitation irresistible. Nevertheless, accepting Dashwood's sponsorship of a reformed edition of a prayer book would seem indiscreet. But it was in keeping with the pragmatic approach toward religion which Franklin had shown ever since, as a youth, he had pointed out to his father that saying grace over meat while it was still in the barrel would be a great time saver as compared with saying grace over a portion at a time in a long succession of meals.

Arguing for his revised version of the *Book of Common Prayer*, Franklin said, "It has often been observed and complained of, that the morning and evening services, as practiced in England and elsewhere, are so long, and filled with so many repetitions, that the continued attention suitable to so serious a duty becomes impracticable, the mind wanders, and the fervency of devotion is slackened." He also said, "Many pious and devout persons, whose age or infirmities will not suffer them to remain for hours in a cold church, especially in the winter season, are obliged to forgo the comfort and edification they would receive by their attendance at divine service." And he said that young people "would probably more frequently, as well as cheerfully, attend divine service if they were not detained so long at any one time."

Franklin reduced the Apostle's Creed by more than half, presenting it as: "I believe in God the Father Almighty, Maker of Heaven and earth; and in Jesus Christ, his son, our Lord. I believe in the Holy Ghost, the forgiveness of sins, and the life everlasting." He condensed many Psalms, and discarded some, to eliminate repetition. He also excised other portions "which, relating to the ancestors of the Jews, were more interesting to them than to us."

After completing his revision of the *Book of Common Prayer*, Franklin revised the Lord's Prayer to read:

Heavenly Father, may all revere thee, and become thy dutiful children and faithful subjects. May thy laws be obeyed on earth as perfectly as they are in Heaven. Provide for us this day as Thou has daily done. Forgive us our trespasses and enable us likewise to forgive those that offend us. Keep us out of temptation, and deliver us from evil.

HE SAID that he substituted "Heavenly Father" for "Our Father which art in Heaven" because his version was "more concise, equally expressive, and better modern English." He substituted "May all revere thy name" for "Hallowed be thy name" because he attributed the earlier version to the influence of the ancient Jewish taboo against pronouncing "the proper or peculiar name of God." "The word *hallowed*," he asserted, "is almost obsolete."

When Franklin died, Dr. Benjamin Rush, the eminent Philadelphia physician, reported that the great man had "desired in his will" that the inscription comparing himself to an old book awaiting translation into a new edition be inscribed on his tombstone. By this request, Rush said, "he has declared his belief in the Christian doctrine of a resurrection." But the doctor was mistaken. Franklin had substituted for his earlier composition a brief, commonplace epitaph.

There are, however, clues that are perhaps more meaningful. In June 1787, when the Constitutional Convention that produced the foundation of U.S. government was deadlocked, Franklin rose to call for daily prayer and said:

The longer I live, the more convincing proofs I see of this truth, that God governs in the affairs of men. And if a sparrow cannot fall to the ground without his notice, is it probable that an empire can rise without his aid? We have been assured, Sir, in the sacred writings, that 'except the Lord build the house, they labor in vain that build it.' I firmly believe this; and I also believe that, without his concurring aid, we shall succeed in this political building no better than the builders of Babel.

If the statement can be taken at face value—and the earnestness argues for such acceptance—we seem to have strong evidence that at the height of his career Franklin believed in a far more personal God than the tenets of Deism would allow. But knowing Franklin's pragmatic penchant, there is room for a lingering suspicion that he just may have thought that the end justified the means.

A more reliable indication of the character of Franklin's faith during his last years is the letter that he wrote three months before his death to Ezra Stiles, president of Yale, a fellow scholar and liberal thinker. In part, Franklin said:

Here is my creed. I believe in one God, Creator of the Universe. That he governs it by his Providence. That he ought to be worshiped. That the most acceptable service we render to him is doing good to his other children. That the soul of man is immortal, and will be treated with justice in another life respecting its conduct in this. These I take to be the fundamental principles of all sound religion, and I regard them as you do in whatever sect I meet with them.

There exists at least one statement indicating that, near the end of his life, Franklin had managed to reconcile to his own satisfaction the laws of science and the promptings of religious faith. The passage is in a letter which he wrote to George Whatley, a man of few religious convictions to be either ruffled or massaged by anything the great man said. Of God, Franklin wrote:

When I observe that there is great frugality, as well as wisdom, in his works, since he has been evidently sparing both of labor and materials; for by the various wonderful inventions of propagation, he has provided for the continual peopling his world with plants and animals, without being at the trouble of repeated new creations; and by the natural reduction of compound substances to their original elements, capable of being employed in new compositions, he has prevented the necessity of creating new matter; so that the earth, water, air, and perhaps, fire, which being compounded from wood, do, when the wood is dissolved, return, and again become air, earth, fire, and water; I say, that, when I see nothing annihilated, and not even a drop of water wasted, I cannot suspect the annihilation of souls, or believe, that he will suffer the daily waste of millions of minds ready made that now exist, and put himself to the continual trouble of making new ones. Thus finding myself to exist in the World, I believe I shall, in some shape or other, always exist.

4

James Madison

THE man writing the letter looked younger than his twenty-two years. He might easily have been taken for a teenager. Not that he looked younger because he was a robust image of rosy-cheeked health. Far from it. A wan face topped the frail body that weighed a hundred pounds or less and stretched to only a few inches over five feet when he stood up between intervals of writing.

From the self-conscious elevation of five years' seniority, he was writing to a friend who had just graduated from college at the age of seventeen. He expressed the hope that his youthful companion would resist "the allurements and vanities that beset us on our first entrance on the theater of life." He acknowledged that "strong desires and great hopes instigate us to arduous enterprises, fortitude and perseverance," but warned that these factors must not seduce us away from eternal truths. "A watchful eye," he wrote, "must be kept on ourselves, lest while we are building renown and bliss here, we neglect to have our names enrolled in the annals of Heaven."

The tone of the letter was serious when the writer considered his friend's prospects, melancholy when he discussed his own. "As to myself," he said, "I am too dull and infirm now to look out for any extraordinary things in this world, for I think my sensations for many months past have intimated to me not to expect a long or healthy life; yet it may be better with me after some time, though I hardly dare expect it, and therefore have little spirit and alacrity to set about anything that is difficult in acquiring and useless in possessing after one has exchanged time for eternity."

Three years after this farewell to earthly scenes, the young man was a member of the Virginia Constitutional Convention that adopted a constitution as the colony became a commonwealth, approved the most eloquent bill of rights in world history, and boldly instructed Virginia's congressmen to introduce a resolution for American independence. After four more years, at the age of twenty-nine, he himself was a congressman. At thirty-four, his wise, skillful, and tireless leadership in a national convention earned him a major place in history as "father of the Constitution of the United States." Meanwhile his scholarship won him membership in the American Philosophical Society; and with a few contributions from John Jay, he and Alexander Hamilton coauthored at white-hot speed a series of essays constituting *The Federalist*, a powerful force for ratification of the U.S. Constitution and one of the world's handful of greatest classics in the field of government.

Subsequently, he would become under Jefferson one of the foremost secretaries of state in American history and afterward for two terms president of the United States. Not least of his accomplishments in some people's eyes was his making such an impression on

Dolley Payne Todd, often called the most charming woman in the United States, that only four months after they first met, *she* proposed marriage.

What transformed James Madison—for of course he was the sickly and despairing young man—into the energetic and determined leader who became one of the most influential of America's Founding Fathers? And what was the nature of his illness? Both questions remain mysteries. John C. Payne, Dolley Madison's brother, once wrote that James Madison was prevented from serving in the military forces during the Revolution by "a constitutional liability to sudden attacks of the nature of epilepsy." He scratched out the last four words and substituted "of a character and effect which suspended his powers of action." Some of Madison's Princeton classmates believed that his completing two academic years in one had made him vulnerable to a constitutional weakness.

Whatever the nature of his malady, he recovered sufficiently to lead one of the world's most valuable lives. And an amazingly full life it was too, crowded with action of national and international significance, enriched by deep scholarship and creative contemplation, blessed by remarkable friendships and a great love—a life lasting eighty-five years, an extraordinary length for his generation.

We may never completely solve the mystery of his illness and apparent recovery. But through all of his adult life, from languishing youth to venerated sage, there runs at least one connecting thread—an intense interest in religion.

What early influences brought Madison to such an intense and consistent lifetime interest? His father was a vestryman of the Anglican Church, but the role was not comparable to that of a Methodist steward, a Presbyterian elder, or Baptist deacon. In colonial days, vestrymen were charged with community responsibilities in addition to those strictly related to the church. For instance, the administration of the poor laws (regulations for the indigent) was one of their tasks. Because of the important civic functions of the vestry, christened but unconfirmed Anglicans were sometimes appointed to it. Therefore the mere fact that Madison's father was a vestryman is not prima facie evidence that he was more religious than the general run of men in his time.

Nevertheless, the family was at least conventionally religious, and there is a persistent tradition that the elder Madison and other close relatives insisted on fair treatment for dissenters. The tradition is bolstered by the fact that in 1771, while the twenty-one-year-old James was a college student, and in a period when Baptists were stoned and jailed in neighboring counties, the first Virginia Baptist Association convened in safety a few miles from the Madisons' home.

Of course, in his pre-college years, James Madison studied under an Anglican minister; but so did most other sons of the Virginia gentry, with no discernible effect on their future piety. Some people have sought significance in the fact that, instead of matriculating at the Anglican-administered College of William and Mary in Virginia, he entered the College of New Jersey (later Princeton University), which was headed by John Witherspoon, a prominent Presbyterian clergyman. Some have speculated that this association both strengthened Madison's religiosity and aroused his distrust of Anglican domination in America. In any event, it was unusual at the time for a Virginian to choose the New Jersey institution in preference to the more convenient and venerable college in Williamsburg. A writer in the *Virginia Gazette* of June 28, 1786, said that there was "but one man educated out of the state, who either has already risen, or promises to rise, much above a state of mediocrity." That single exception was a Virginia legislator, James Madison. Late in life, Madison said that the effect of the lowland environment on his health had caused him to look beyond Williamsburg for an education.

If he was both deeply religious and suspicious of bishops, as he seems to have been even as an adolescent, there was nothing about Princeton to discourage these tendencies. Fellow students later remembered both his piety and his witty sallies against some aspects of the established church. From his Virginia home at the age of twenty-one, after completing his studies at Princeton, he wrote on November 9, 1772, to William Bradford, his closest college friend:

> I think you made a judicious choice of history and the science of morals for your winter's study. They seem to be of the most universal benefit to men of sense and taste in every post, and must certainly be of great use to youth in settling the principles and refining the judgment, as well as in enlarging knowledge and correcting the imagination. I doubt not but you design to season them with a divinity now and then, which, like the philosopher's stone, in the hands of a good man, will turn them and every lawful acquirement into the nature of itself, and make them more precious than fine gold.

Few would have guessed that the writer of those lines had been neither confirmed in the Anglican Church nor affiliated with any other Christian sect. During his postgraduate days at Princeton, he had studied, among other subjects, theology. Back home in Virginia, he pursued, on his own, further studies in both theology and law. Nevertheless, he believed that, even if his health problems should ease, his weak voice would debar him from both the legal profession and the ministry. He studied theology for the reasons that he had urged it upon Bradford. As for the law, he said it was "a sort of general lover that woos all the graces." And on December 1, 1773, he wrote Bradford that he had "procured books" for legal studies, explaining, "The principles and modes of government are too important to be disregarded by an inquisitive mind and I think are well worth a critical examination by all students that have health and leisure."

Perhaps he had a half-submerged hope that, despite current problems of voice and health, someday he just might be able to enter upon one profession or the other. In urging Bradford to prepare himself to some extent for each of these pursuits in case he should choose to embrace either of them after an early career in other things, he may have been echoing his own desires.

Though he had not taken the first step of formal affiliation with any denomination, he was quite evidently committed to Christianity. Praising theology as "the most sublime of all sciences," he said:

> I have sometimes thought there could not be a stronger testimony in favor of Religion against Temporal enjoyments even the most rational and manly than for men who occupy the most honorable and gainful departments and are rising in reputation and wealth, publicly to declare their unsatisfactoriness by becoming fervent advocates in the cause of Christ, and I wish you may give in your evidence in this way.

At the time that Madison wrote those words, he already was engaged in studies that would lead him away from orthodoxy as it was understood in his day. While a student at the Rev. Mr. Witherspoon's Princeton, he had secretly read Voltaire. He was not a follower of the Frenchman, but he resented any attempt to censor his own reading and was determined to explore all fields of philosophical inquiry. After graduation, he continued to read French skeptics but was not sympathetic to their views. In a letter of December 1, 1773, he confided to Bradford that he subscribed to London reviews filled with quotations from French philosophers and their English followers. He expected to continue to read these journals even though he wrote, "I find them loose in their principles, encouragers of free enquiry even such as destroys the most essential truths, enemies to serious religion and extremely partial in their citations, seeking them rather to justify their censures and commendations than to give the reader a just specimen of the author's genius." The implication is that Madison, like many young intellectuals, thought it his responsibility to keep abreast of the currents of heterodoxy but would not recommend a testing of the waters to less mature minds.

As a student at Princeton, he had been exposed to the reality of those old spelling bee favorites—disestablishmentarianism and antidisestablishmentarianism. Though reared in the Anglican Church, which was the official state church in both England and Virginia, he believed in the separation of church and state. In student campaigns and programs, he voiced his opposition to a state church. Sometimes he expressed his views in language that some of his elders, including some who shared his views, considered scurrilous.

As a young man, even when he had scarcely attained his majority, he sometimes used a style that was downright preachy. He wrote like a Founding Father long before he was one. Phrases appropriate to an elder statesman sounded priggish and pompous when they flowed from the pen of one who seemed even younger than his tender years.

But this was only one side of his personality. Intimate friends testified to the sparkle of his dinner table wit. When the company was exclusively male, his humor frequently was risqué. He may never have completely quit his habit of pontificating in measured phrases, but eventually what had been irritating in a stripling became appropriate to a mature statesman famed for wisdom.

Madison's initial aversion to Enlightenment writings challenging religious orthodoxy yielded by degrees to a growing acceptance of Deism. As frequently happens, the middle-aged Madison would have been impatient with any young man voicing some of the views that he himself had expressed at the same age. But—and this is extremely important—he would have defended the right of the young man, or anyone else, to express those same opinions. Not only was an intense interest in religion an unbroken thread running through his life; a perpetual strand of that thread was his devotion to religious liberty.

Anglicans, though they became increasingly impatient with what they considered British exploitation of the North American colonies, still remained true to their denomination. But the troubles between the mother country and the colonists led others to break with their church or at least advocate its disestablishment. At Princeton, Madison joined those calling for separation of church and state. Back in Virginia, he continued to advocate the same principle and did not cease his labors until it prevailed. After that accomplishment, he was a zealous guardian of religious freedom.

As a member of the Virginia Constitutional Convention of 1776, and of its committee, which drafted the Declaration of Rights, he was a molding force in composing the article on religious freedom. As a member of Virginia's first state legislature, successor to the old colonial Assembly, he continued to speak up for that principle. In 1777, the voters of his district did not return him to his post. Apparently they were not particularly riled about his stand on religious freedom or any other major issue, but were angered by his refusal to follow the tradition of providing alcoholic beverages for the voters on election day. He seemed to cling to the eccentric notion that a clear head was desirable when a citizen exercised the responsibility of choice.

In Virginia, as in other colonies and in England itself, the opposing legislative candidates always knew how each citizen voted. Each voter in turn publicly declared his allegiance to a particular candidate. The recipient of the vote then shook hands with his supporter and thanked him. The colonists were always self-consciously proclaiming themselves successors to the ancient Greeks and Romans. In voting, they preferred the public openness of the Athenians to the secret ballot of the Romans. Most were inclined to agree with Cicero, who fought the secret ballot when that reform was adopted in his time and maintained that it was an invitation to covert action of a dishonest nature.

Despite Madison's failure at the polls in 1777, later that year he was elected to the Council of State and in 1779 to the Continental Congress. After expiration of his congressional term, Madison was elected to the Virginia House of Delegates, lower chamber of the state legislature. Service on its committee on religion gave him the opportunity to advance religious freedom in his native Virginia, most populous of the American states. He called for disestablishment of the Episcopal (Anglican) Church and, supported by the Baptists and soon the Presbyterians as well, opposed the continuation of tax assessments to support the long-favored denomination. When Patrick Henry sought to subvert Madison's efforts by offering state financial support to Methodists, Presbyterians, and Baptists as well as Episcopalians, the Baptists refused, closely followed by the Presbyterians, leaders of these two denominations asserting that if special privileges for Episcopalians were wrong, state-decreed advantages for their own churches were equally unjust.

Madison was always nervous when speaking in public. Some people think that it was this discomfort that impelled him to be excused from graduation exercises at Princeton. It is possible that the epileptic-like attacks that had made him so uncertain of the future as a young man, though later they may have abated a great deal, continued to threaten him with embarrassment whenever he consented to participate in a public proceeding.

Whatever the cause of his apprehension about public speaking, his doubts were conquered by his zeal for national union and civil rights, especially religious freedom. In the Virginia legislature, he began his fight to deprive the Episcopal Church of special privileges with a bold speech from the floor, presenting a resolution that if it had been adopted would immediately have disestablished that institution, leaving it at once to fend for itself like all the other churches in Virginia. In his successful fight to end tax support for that or any other denomination, he was courageous and indefatigable. Thomas Jefferson was the author of the great Virginia Statute for Religious Freedom, whose memorable phrases have inspired people in virtually every civilized nation, but it was Madison who carried it to final passage. Though the Virginia Plan, which made possible the formation of the federal republic, was presented to the national constitutional convention by Edmund Randolph, then governor of the Old Dominion, Madison was the author of it. He also pushed it through that assemblage, being despite his discomfort one of the three most frequent speakers.

He not only wrote *Federalist* essays that helped to persuade people in all of the thirteen states to support ratification of the Constitution, but in the Virginia convention for ratification confronted the greatest orator in America, Patrick Henry. Madison had a weak and unimpressive voice and a far-from-commanding presence. When he spoke, he used notes concealed in his hat. Grasping it with both hands, as if it were a ship's wheel, the intrepid little captain of Virginia's ratification forces steered the measure through all the reefs of legislative resistance.

Madison's unwavering support of ratification cost him the votes of many of his constituents and paved the way for his defeat in a race for U.S. senator. But no temptations of wealth, power, or public esteem could lure him from the path of duty.

His determined, lifelong opposition to slavery also cost him support and perhaps some personal friendships. But, though a master of compromise in negotiation, he would not compromise on what he regarded as a major moral issue.

After the Constitution became the law of the land, Madison labored effectively to add to it a bill of rights. He was particularly concerned about religious freedom, echoing his earlier statements in the Virginia legislature that it was not a matter of toleration but of right.

As secretary of state in Jefferson's cabinet, he supported from personal conviction as well as loyalty the president's insistence that nations should be obedient to the same moral standards by which an individual was judged.

As president of the United States, Madison completely subordinated his popularity and prestige to the demands of the nation's welfare. Realizing that he had to deal with a Congress intensely jealous of executive initiative, he asked some friendly members of the House and Senate to initiate measures for national defense to which he could submit with feigned reluctance. He played his part so unselfishly that Americans in his own time and in subsequent generations regarded him as a weak leader pushed by bold legislators. Indeed, that estimate prevailed even among prominent scholars until the 1950s and 1960s, when volumes V and VI of Irving Brant's great biography revealed the fourth president's patriotic sacrifice of his own reputation.

A frequently overlooked aspect of Madison's presidency, his emphasis on religious freedom, is cited by Edwin S. Gaustad in his insightful *Neither King nor Prelate: Religion and the New Nation, 1776–1826*. As chief executive, Madison advocated an even more rigid separation of church and state than Jefferson called for. In 1811, Madison warned that an act of Congress incorporating the Protestant Episcopal Church in Alexandria in the District of Columbia could open the door to a dangerous union of civil and religious authority. He saw this danger as particularly great because the church planned to resume the colonial responsibility of Anglican churches in Virginia to dispense charity to the needy and provide education for the poor. Likewise, he vetoed a bill that would have provided land for a Baptist church in the Mississippi Territory, saying that it comprised "a precedent for the appropriation of funds of the United States for the use and support of religious societies." He even questioned whether "the appointment of chaplains to the two houses of Congress [was] consistent with the pure principle of religious freedom." Later he declared unequivocally, "The establishment of the chaplainship to Congress is a palpable violation of equal rights, as well as of Constitutional principles."

Sometimes Madison praised the influence of religion, and sometimes he decried ecclesiastical threats to liberty; but he never underestimated the importance of religion. In an age when some Enlightenment leaders wrote of religion as a remnant sure to retreat from the world before an advancing science, Madison's unwavering insistence on religion's eternal importance bolstered the faith of many.

His faith could not be ascribed to intellectual deficiency. Among his compatriots, though not quite as versatile as either Jefferson or Franklin, Madison was also a Renaissance man. No American was more versed in the governments of ancient, medieval, and modern times. Besides vast erudition, he had brought innovative genius to political science. Few laymen, or for that matter clergymen, were so well grounded in theology. From early days, he was well read in "polite literature." As a mature statesman, he studied natural history. He asked Jefferson to recommend some texts on chemistry and to select laboratory equipment for him. Though Jefferson and Franklin left behind written work in theology and philosophy, neither approached those subjects in the systematic way that Madison did.

Madison's sense of history brought a wide perspective to his study of contemporary society. Jefferson and Franklin had the same advantage. But he had an additional one: his theological sense of time gave him a long view beyond the oldest annals of humankind.

He did not make his observations as exciting to the average person as did Jefferson and Franklin. But those with whom this shy man felt at ease were treated to an engagingly frank conversational feast as nutritious as it was appealing. One of the favored ones was Jefferson, whose friendship had begun when Madison's parents had consulted him on the education of their college-bound son. Another was Margaret Bayard Smith. The famous diarist visited him in 1835 when at the age of eighty-four he was afflicted by various illnesses and had been forced by financial problems, resulting in large part from the borrowings of his wastrel stepson, to sell part of his beloved farm and adopt a more spartan lifestyle. Like other good friends, she found him not at all embittered but still loyal to the ideals of his youth. His conversation, she said, was "a stream of history . . . so rich in sentiments and facts, so enlivened by anecdotes and epigrammatic remarks, so frank and confidential as to opinions and measures, that it had an interest and charm which the conversation of few men now living could have. . . . His little blue eyes sparkled like stars from under his bushy gray eyebrows and amidst the deep wrinkles of his poor thin face." But she said that, "had a single stranger or indifferent person been present," Madison "would have been mute."

Madison had a firm faith that grew from orthodoxy in his early years to something more complex in later ones. There is no detailed record of his beliefs, but certain things we do know. He was no atheist. His morals were orthodoxly Christian, but he was free of any bigoted assumption that adherents of other religions were automatically morally inferior. His reason told him that the truth was otherwise. Reason was reinforced by the gratitude with which he recalled how Haym Salomon, a patriotic Jew, by lending money without charging interest, had helped him and other delegates to the Continental Congress to continue their duties without pay. Madison also held fast to the idea that nothing in life was more important than religion and that religion could never become irrelevant. If he did not believe these things, he was one of the greatest hypocrites in American history. Those who knew him well believed this impossible.

5

John Adams

I NEVER write or talk upon divinity. I have had more than I could do of humanity." This seemingly cynical comment appears in a letter from John Adams to his beloved wife, Abigail. The opinion sets Adams apart from leading Enlightenment thinkers of Europe who dreamed of the perfectibility of man. It also distanced the New Englander from such fellow Americans as Benjamin Franklin and Thomas Jefferson, who sometimes believed that near perfection was attainable by many of humankind.

Adams wrote that statement in 1800, an unhappy and stressful year for him. It was then that, trying for a second term as president of the United States, he lost to Thomas Jefferson. The campaign had been a disgusting one of vilification by adherents of each of the two candidates. The loss of support in Pennsylvania had helped to deprive Adams of the needed majority. He attributed the defeat in that key state to the writings of a notorious journalist, James Callender. This man had charged that Adams, upon becoming president, had imported two mistresses, one from France and one from Germany. While retaining the French charmer, however, Adams supposedly had returned her rival to her native Germany.

The Pennsylvania Germans were incensed, not so much by reports of sexual immorality as by the thought that the president would reject a fräulein while holding fast to a mademoiselle. There was no foundation for the scandalous story circulated by Callender, but as a hired pen for some Republican politicians, he had accomplished his purpose. Shortly, angered by what he considered the ingratitude of Jefferson, he turned upon the newly elected president and made the most of a rumored liaison between him and his slave Sally Hemings.

But this was no help to the ousted incumbent, who continued to smart at the misuse of his name in print. Few people today know that there were once such charges against Adams. One look at the Gilbert Stuart portrait of 1823 with the turned-down mouth and deeply etched lines of disapproval has been sufficient to discourage generations of Americans from imagining the old New Englander frolicking with imported mistresses of any nationality. The Stuart portrait is a brilliant psychological study, in which Adams's intelligence and strong character shine through the vanity and irritability. But the look of self-conscious rectitude is not one that any casting director would assign to a scandalous sexual adventurer.

But in the heat of a presidential campaign, almost anything is believable. Adams not only lamented his loss of office but also despaired over loss of reputation. It was all so unfair, but also predictably human. Sometimes people seemed to wallow in muck with the sensual satisfaction of hogs.

But if Adams had little faith in the character of his fellow humans, he fairly enough also despaired of raising his own character to anything remotely approaching perfection. As has been pointed out by Paul C. Nagel, one of the most insightful of Adams biographers in our time, his attitude was largely a reflection of his Puritan background. His theology and philosophy were not nearly so much influenced by philosophers of the Age of Reason as by the Puritan and Calvinist doctrines inculcated by various relatives, among them his father, who wanted him to become a clergyman.

These teachings always began and ended with the doctrine of original sin, the belief that, in disobeying God, Adam had incurred a burden of guilt transmitted to all his descendants in the entire human race. "In Adam's fall, we sinned all," said the *New England Primer*, the reading text for generations of little New Englanders. Though Adams eventually seemed to move away from a literal interpretation of the Garden of Eden, he seemed convinced of its symbolic truth. Apparently he always believed that, like all the rest of humanity, he was guilty of sin against God. This belief did not protect Adams from the temptations of vanity. He sometimes suffered pangs of jealousy not only over the successes of enemies but even when Washington and others that he admired seemed to receive excessive praise. And he worried greatly about symbols of distinction. As vice president of the United States presiding over the Senate, he reminded its members that, although the President was officially addressed as "Your Excellency," no similar title had been adopted for the number two man. He was wounded in spirit when an irreverent senator, eyeing Adams's roly-poly figure, proposed "Your Rotundity."

Neither did Calvinism make Adams immune to the temptations of the flesh. His private writings are filled with erotic analogies. It is not that they include many risqué references. It is rather that a landscape's curves were likely to suggest to him those of a woman's body. He was more likely to see in a cloud the shape of a woman's breast than to find it "very like a whale." Once when he was courting his future wife, bad weather prevented his calling on her. His subsequent note to her suggested that the missed engagement was perhaps for the best; he implied in a lightly veiled code that, had he been with her, he might have had difficulty controlling his amorous desires.

Again and again, he was almost drunk with heady ambition and vainglory, only to be plunged upon self-examination into shame and severe melancholy. Once he confessed, "I muse, I mope, I ruminate—I am often in Reveries and Brown studies." Excited over his opportunity to found a dynasty of power, he warned his young son John Quincy, "You come into life with advantages which will disgrace you if your success is mediocre. And if you do not rise to the head not only of your profession, but of your country, it will be owing to your own laziness, slovenliness, and obstinacy." Yet he viewed with horror his own willingness to sacrifice so much, perhaps even his children's happiness, for the attainment of worldly goals. He lamented "that men find ways to persuade themselves to believe any absurdity, to submit to any prostitution, rather than forgo their wishes and desires; their reason becomes at last an eloquent advocate on the side of their passions and [they] bring themselves to believe that black is white, that vice is virtue, that folly is wisdom and eternity a moment."

Adams's survey of the temptations of life was often exhilarating, but his sober analysis of them was predictably depressing. One is reminded of the retort of the Rt. Rev. William A. Brown, Episcopal Bishop of Southern Virginia, to a Calvinist clergyman chiding him about some foibles of the old gentleman's flock. "A Presbyterian," the prelate said, "will do anything an Episcopalian would. He just won't enjoy it."

Though Adams seems to have thought about religion in connection with everything he considered seriously, he did not regard the Bible as the only repository of divinely inspired writing. Some of his contemporaries, like some medieval churchmen, conceded a measure of divine inspiration to a few great classical writers, such as Virgil. But their pale penumbra was seen as merely a forecast of the bright dawn of the Hebrew prophets and their Christian successors. Adams, on the other hand, ascribed to some ancient Greek and Roman writers a prescience equal to that of some of the Biblical prophets.

Faith in aristocracy was almost a religious tenet with Adams. In support of it, he quoted to Jefferson some lines from Theognis, first presenting the original Greek and then following with his own translation: "When we want to purchase horses, asses, or rams, we inquire for the wellborn. And everyone wishes to procure from the good breeds. A good man does not care to marry a shrew, the daughter of a shrew, unless they give him a great deal of money with her."

Adams added his own comment:

Theognis lived five hundred and forty-four years before Jesus Christ. Has science, or morals, or philosophy, or criticism or Christianity, advanced or improved, or enlightened mankind upon this subject, and shown them that the idea of the "well born" is a prejudice, a phantasm, a point no point, a gape fly away, a dream? I say it is the ordinance of God Almighty, in the Constitution of human nature and wrought into the fabric of the universe.

Few people were ever so emphatic as an aroused John Adams. He told Jefferson, "If you deny any one of these positions, I will prove them to demonstration by examples from your own Virginia, and from every other state in the Union, and from the history of every nation civilized and savage, from all we know of the time of the creation of the world."

Apparently Adams also believed that post-Biblical writings could be divinely inspired. Immediately following his citation of Theognis, he summoned in support of the same proposition Justice Sir Thomas Littleton, the great fifteenth-century author of *Tenures*. "Born of a noble race, a gentleman born," Adams translated from Littleton's legal French. And he added, "We may call this sentiment a prejudice, because we can give what names we please to such things as we please; but in my opinion it is a part of the natural history of man, and politicians and philosophers may as well project to make the animal live without bones or blood as society can pretend to establish a free government without attention to it." Apparently there was a smidgin of Shintoism in Adams's religion.

His sense of family heritage actually buttressed his revolutionary spirit. Merrill Peterson, in *Adams and Jefferson: A Revolutionary Dialogue*, shrewdly observed, "Adams reconstructed the Puritan past into a legend of republican beginnings, thereby conscripting it in the cause of revolution."

Adams saw an intimate relationship between his family's faith and its record of citizenship. In a letter on July 19, 1812, to Benjamin Rush, he said, "What has preserved this race of Adamses in all their ramifications in such numbers, health, peace, comfort, and mediocrity? I believe it is religion, without which they would have been rakes, fops, sots, gamblers, starved with hunger, or frozen with cold, scalped by Indians, etc., etc., etc., been melted away and disappeared."

Though some Puritan families loved the arts and even left behind portraits in elaborate dress, Adams's particular brand of the faith inhibited his aesthetic development. From Paris, he wrote Abigail:

> The public buildings and gardens, the paintings, sculpture, architecture, music, etc., of these cities have already filled many volumes. But what is all this to me? I receive but little pleasure in beholding all these things because I cannot but consider them as bagatelles, introduced by time and luxury in exchange for the great qualities and hardy, manly virtues of the human heart. I cannot help suspecting that the more elegance, the less virtue, in all times and countries.

Adams's impatience with orthodox preachers may have been increased by the awareness that his father-in-law, a member of that tribe, had hoped that his daughter, Adams's beloved Abigail, would break her engagement to this young lawyer with unorthodox notions. Though the situation troubled Abigail, it also stimulated her wry sense of humor. Her father had promised each of his daughters that she would have the privilege of selecting the text for his first sermon after her marriage. When Abigail's turn came, she chose, "John came neither eating nor drinking, and ye say, He hath a devil."

John Adams was a man of powerful prejudices, and one of the strongest early in his career was against young followers of the profession that his family had urged upon him. He said, "People are not disposed to inquire for piety, integrity, good sense or learning in a young preacher, but for stupidity (for so I must call the pretended sanctity of some absolute dunces) [and for] irresistible grace and original sin." Resolved to pursue a legal career, he said, "If I can gain the honor of treading in the rear, and silently admiring the noble and gallant achievements of the foremost rank, I shall think myself worthy of a louder triumph than if I headed the whole army of orthodox preachers." Such opinions attracted considerable attention in Massachusetts, where orthodox ministers for generations had constituted an exalted governing class and still enjoyed more prestige than followers of other professions.

Adams's attitude toward the clergy did not soften with the years. In 1817, at the age of eighty-two, he wrote to Jefferson: "Twenty times in the course of my late readings, have I been on the point of breaking out, 'This would be the best of all worlds if there were no religion in it!' But in this exclamation I should have been . . . fanatical. . . . Without religion, this world would be something not fit to be mentioned in polite company—I mean hell."

But he did not completely despair of the clergy, even those he regarded as most fanatical. He continued:

So far from believing in the total and universal depravity of human nature, I believe there is no individual totally depraved. The most abandoned scoundrel that ever existed never wholly extinguished his conscience, and while conscience remains there is some religion. Popes, Jesuits, Sarbonnists, and Inquisitors have some religion. Fears and terrors appear to have produced a universal credulity—but fears of pain and death here do not seem so unconquerable as fears of what is to come hereafter.

It is interesting to note that in these two quotations, both from the same paragraph, Adams first attacks religion as detrimental to the world and then cites it as a redeeming force in the lives of those he regards as fanatical enemies of humanity. One of the things that adds to the interest of Adams's correspondence, aside from his wide knowledge and occasionally vivid phrases, is the vehemence with which he makes a sweeping assertion and the abruptness with which he contradicts it in the interest of moderation. His letters are not carefully edited missives but overheard conversations.

Commenting on the doctrine of eternal damnation for great sinners, Adams revealed both his departure from orthodoxy and his belief in, and love for, a benevolent God. Of eternal damnation, he said, "I believe in no such thing." He explained, "My adoration of the author of the universe is too profound and too sincere. The love of God and his creation—delight, joy, triumph, exultation in my own existence—though but an atom, a *molecule organique*, in the universe—these are my religion."

He also declared his disbelief in demoniacal possession, faith in which had once led to orgiastic witch hunts in his native Massachusetts. Anticipating the anger his declaration would provoke in some quarters, he wrote, "Howl, snarl, bite, ye Calvinistic, ye Athanasian divines, if ye will. Ye will say I am no Christian. I say ye are no Christians, and there the account is balanced. Yet I believe all the honest men among you are Christians in my sense of the word."

Adams said he did believe in revelation. But his discussion of it showed that for him the word had a meaning different from that intended by the orthodox of his day. "The human understanding," he said, "is a revelation from its maker, and can never be disputed or doubted." And he also said, "No miracles, no prophecies are necessary to prove celestial communication."

John Adams is seen at his best and most appealing in his relationship with Abigail. Their personal correspondence during his diplomatic service abroad, and at other times when his public duties kept them apart, leaves no doubt of the close and enduring nature of their relationship. Abigail was a woman of liberal political sentiments who advocated the vote for women, but her religious orientation was more conservative than her husband's, though not quite so traditional as her preacher father's. But she never seems to have feared that John was unsaved nor to have thought of him as un-Christian. Nevertheless, she found comfort in a more personal God than he envisioned.

Late in life, after reading his son John Quincy Adams's letters to his own children, John was disturbed by the casual assurance with which John Quincy had admonished his progeny to follow "the Biblic rule of faith." The old man exploded, "The Biblic Rule of Faith! What Bible? King James? The Hebrews'?" There were, he said, "thirty thousand variations" in the different versions. To which one did John Quincy refer? As on many other occasions, the senior Adams "generated more indignation than he could properly contain." Vehemently he exclaimed, "An incarnate God!!! An eternal, self-existent, omnipotent, omniscient author of this stupendous universe, suffering on a cross!!! My soul starts with horror at the idea, and it has stupefied the Christian world. It has been the source of almost all the corruptions of Christianity."

To Benjamin Rush, Adams wrote, "Ask me not then whether I am a Catholic or Protestant, Calvinist or Armenian. As far as they are Christians, I wish to be a fellow disciple with them all." On November 4, 1815, he wrote to David Sewall, "Translations of the Bible into all languages and sent among all people, I hope, will produce translations into English and French, Spanish and German and Italian of sacred books of Persians, the Chinese, the Hindoos, etc. etc. etc. Then our grandchildren and my great-grandchildren may compare notes and hold fast all that is good." Writing to John

Quincy Adams on November 15, 1816, he called for "universal toleration," saying that if religious freedom prevailed, so would Christianity, augmented by borrowings from other faiths.

Though John Adams had taken pride in John Quincy's achievements ever since the son's youthful precocity, another son, Charles,
brought embarrassment and distress. As a Harvard student, Charles
led a rebellion against the school's officials. On the downward path
of alcoholism, he was surprised while rifling through John Quincy's
papers. A third son, Thomas, from childhood suffered both chronic
physical illness and melancholy and became an alcoholic. Meanwhile, John and Abigail suffered such financial reversal that at times
they feared there would be no estate to leave for their children and
that they themselves would have no home of their own. Amid these
depressing circumstances, John Adams revealed a sustaining faith.
He told John Quincy, "I foresee what all ages have foreseen, that
poor earthly mortals can foresee nothing, and that after all our
studies and anxieties, we must trust Providence."

When Abigail died, John Adams, deeply moved by Jefferson's
letter of condolence, declared that he himself, like his old friend in
Virginia, found a large measure of consolation in belief in the soul's
immortality. He wrote,

> I know not how to prove physically, that we shall meet and
> know each other in a future state; nor does Revelation as I
> can find, give us any positive assurance of such a felicity. My
> reasons for believing it, as I do most undoubtedly, are all
> moral and divine. I believe in God and in his wisdom and
> benevolence; and I cannot conceive that such a being could
> make such a species as the human, merely to live and die on
> this earth. If I did not believe in a future state, I should be-
> lieve in no God. This Universe, this [totality] would appear,
> with all of its swelling pomp, a boyish firework. And if there
> be a future state, why should the Almighty dissolve forever all
> the tender ties which unite us so delightfully in this world,
> and forbid us to see each other in the next?

WHEN ABIGAIL died in 1818, John was eighty-three years old. He died eight years later, on July 4, 1826, the fiftieth anniversary of the Declaration of Independence. His last words were, "Jefferson still sur—." With ample reason, it has been assumed ever since that the last intended word was "survived." Many writers have called attention to the ironic fact that, unknown to Adams, Jefferson himself had died a little earlier on the same national holiday so significant to both.

Adams had looked forward to reunion with Abigail in the afterlife. Jefferson had divulged to him a hope that those who had labored so hard for national independence would meet again in another world in an assemblage reminiscent of their sessions in Philadelphia. Was Adams, in the last moments of his life, reflecting that Jefferson would soon (very soon as gauged by the standards of eternity) join him again in comradeship?

There was irony in Adams's last will and testament as well as in his death. This man, who once had been tempted by the thought that the world might be better off without religion, bequeathed funds to replace the church of which Abigail's orthodox father had been pastor and in which John and Abigail had worshiped.

There was more consistency in Adams's religious transitions than a casual observer might have supposed. In a letter to Benjamin Rush on August 28, 1811, he said, "I have been a church-going animal for seventy-six years, from the cradle." On July 4, 1826, the day of his death, he could have repeated the statement word for word, only amending the number of years from seventy-six to ninety-one.

Calmly accepting the end of life, he had said, "He who loves the Workman and his work, and does what he can to preserve and improve it, shall be accepted of Him."

Charles Francis Adams, John's grandson, perpetuated the family tradition of public service and scholarship, becoming a most effective U.S. minister to Great Britain at the time of the Civil War and later the biographer of his grandfather and editor of his papers. Charles Francis wrote of John Adams's religious attitudes:

He devoted himself to a very elaborate examination of the religion of all ages and nations, the results of which he committed to paper in a desultory manner. The issue of it was the formation of his theological opinions very much in the mold accepted by the Unitarians of New England. Rejecting, with the independent spirit which in early life had driven him from the ministry, the prominent doctrines of Calvinism, the trinity, the atonement and election, he was content to settle down upon the Sermon on the Mount as a perfect code presented to men by a more than mortal teacher.

6

George Washington

GEORGE WASHINGTON was a vestryman, a member of the governing body of his parish church, before he was a communicant of that or any other church. That sort of thing was not customary in colonial Virginia, but it was not unheard of either. Washington worshiped with an Anglican congregation. Anglicans constituted the established church of England and its colonies. The link between church and state was so strong that some of the important functions of local government, such as the administration of the "poor laws" providing care for the indigent, were the responsibility of the vestries. Sometimes men of proven probity and sound judgment who had been christened as infants but had not formally become communicants were elected to vestries because of their fitness for community leadership.

Washington's election to the vestry before he was a communicant testifies to the esteem in which he was held by his neighbors. But what does his disinclination to become a fully participating member of the congregation suggest about his attitude toward religion?

Some mystery surrounds the subject. Diligent researchers have found no evidence of Washington's ever having taken communion, and there are reports of his having declined. His abstention was particularly noticeable when he was accompanied by his wife, because she is reported to have participated invariably.

Many writers have tended to interpret Washington's views on religion in terms of their own predilections. Tim LaHaye, in *The Faith of Our Fathers*, concluded that "were George Washington living today, he would freely identify with the Bible-believing branch of evangelical Christianity that is having such a positive influence on our nation." Franklin Steiner, in *The Religious Beliefs of Our Presidents*, without making a categorical distinction between those generally regarded as great and those considered mediocre, concluded one by one that virtually all of the great ones were freethinkers. As indubitably one of the greatest presidents, Washington was portrayed as one of the most liberal of the freethinkers.

Many writers have placed Washington's religious views at various points between these two poles. His most widely read biographer was Mason Locke Weems, a conscious mythmaker, the foremost disseminator, if not indeed the creator, of the cherry tree story. He was also the inspirer of the many depictions of Washington kneeling in prayer in the snows of Valley Forge. Weems wrote that a Quaker named Potts, coming upon the general on his knees in the winter white as he addressed an appeal to his Maker, told his own wife, "If George Washington be not a man of God, I am greatly deceived—and still more shall I be deceived if God does not, through him, work out a great salvation for America." The sentence that Weems attributed to the semi-anonymous Quaker was at least as stiff as a snow-buried knee and is in the same style used by all the estimable characters in Weems's *Life of George Washington*, including the juvenile George himself replying to an irate father who had lost a prized cherry tree.

Of course, no one can prove that Washington did not kneel in the snow at Valley Forge. But the imagined event is most unlikely. Washington was an idealist, but a very practical one. From his days as a young surveyor, he had endured discomfort in the line of duty but recorded in his journal his pleasure at every opportunity to enjoy a comfortable bed with fresh linen. In freezing weather, he might have enjoyed the protective warmth of a fur coat but would not needlessly have donned a hair shirt.

One writer, in misguided zeal to demonstrate the general's "Christian" behavior, said that when an American officer interrupted Washington in prayer at Valley Forge, the commander, "without rising from his knees," shot the man and "resumed his quiet devotions."

More important than whether Washington would have prayed on his knees, or in a specific setting, is the question of whether he would have prayed at all. Many of his associates were Deists, and many Deists considered praying a waste of time. But we know that some others, though having no hope of diverting God from a predetermined course, believed that prayer had value as a conduit to obtain divine inspiration. Washington quite conceivably went farther than this. He believed that the Deity intervened in human affairs. Therefore, it would not have been inconsistent for him to petition for such intervention. There are reports of his praying at various stages of his life. Some people have pointed out that virtually all of these witnesses favored prayer, but that fact does not necessarily invalidate their testimony. Skepticism is merited in cases where the national hero is made to sound like an animated sectarian tract, but in other instances automatic rejection is as subjective as unquestioning acceptance.

There is ample indication of Washington's belief in life after death. Peter R. Henriques presents some of the evidence in a particularly insightful article ("The Final Struggle between George Washington and the Grim King," *The Virginia Magazine of History and Biography*, vol. 107, pp. 73–97). When Patsy Custis, his young stepdaughter, died after years of epileptic torture, Washington declared his belief that she had gone to "a more happy and peaceful abode." Henriques sees in this comment no evidence of Washington's faith in the possibility of a happy afterlife but rather an assertion that the afflicted girl was at last free from pain, possibly at the expense of awareness. This seems unlikely: The general, when writing on a serious topic, habitually chose his words carefully. If he had meant simply to imply that she was "out of her misery" or "better off dead," he assuredly would have said so. Instead he viewed death not only as her escape from her life's trials but also as a gift of happiness rewarding her for a conscientious life. Further confirmation of his attitude is found in his writing after the death of a favorite niece that "she must be happy because her virtue has a claim to it." Here Washington obviously envisioned a blissful afterlife for those whose earthly existence had been innocent.

Another hint of Washington's thoughts about immortality is afforded by a letter that he addressed to a favorite female correspondent, Mrs. Annis Boudinot Stockton, on August 31, 1788. "With Cicero in speaking respecting his belief of the immortality of the soul," he wrote, "I will say, if I am in a grateful delusion, it is an innocent one, and I am willing to remain under its influences." The tone seems light, but the seriousness of the next paragraph alerts us not to dismiss this comment as mere banter. Accepting her felicitations on "the present prospect of our public affairs," he says, "I can never trace the concatenation of causes, which led to these events, without acknowledging the mystery and admiring the goodness of Providence. To that superintending power alone is our retraction from the brink of ruin to be attributed."

Washington's statement to Mrs. Stockton about his belief in "immortality of the soul" may seem akin to Blaise Pascal's famous "wager." The great seventeenth-century thinker argued that, as eternal happiness is possible if God exists and one accepts that premise and lives accordingly, whereas nothing is lost under the same assumption if God does not exist, the sensible person will put aside doubts and live in faith. The argument is not as simplistic as the bald statement of it sounds. Pascal, though a great mathematician and scientist, argued that both of these views rested on some unprovable assumptions and that a truly skeptical person might doubt even his or her own existence. In even small matters of daily life, one would be paralyzed by complete skepticism in mundane affairs. Therefore, in religion as in everyday practical matters, one must set aside paralyzing quibbles.

Even when grieving the loss of a loved one, Washington did not question God's justice. When his nephew, George Augustine Washington, was on his deathbed, the president wrote, "The will of Heaven is not to be controverted or scrutinized by the children of this world. It therefore becomes the creatures of it to submit with patience and resignation to the will of the Creator, whether it be to prolong, or to shorten, the number of our days. To bless them with health or afflict them with pain." After the young man's death, Washington confided to a friend, "It is a loss I sincerely regret, but as it is the will of heaven, whose decrees are always just and wise, I submit to it without a murmur."

The general's use of the words "sincerely regret" might suggest that he did not feel deeply the deaths even of those close to him. Such, however, was far from the case. His friends testified to that fact, and upon the death of Nathanel Greene, his old comrade in arms, he confessed that the occasion was so moving that he "could scarce persuade [himself] to touch upon it."

Writing in 1791 to Henry Knox, his secretary of war and Revolutionary comrade in arms, the president sympathized with him on the death of a son. He realistically conceded that "parental feelings are too much alive in the moment of these misfortunes to admit the consolations of religion or philosophy." Nevertheless Washington repeatedly recommended to grieving friends the "comforts of religion and philosophy."

On what philosophy did he rely? Some who have heard that

Washington's formal education consisted of a few years at an "old field school," a one-room affair erected near a conjunction of property lines for the training of planters' children, have assumed that his philosophical foundation was a collection of cracker-barrel homilies. Such was not the case. Washington was not a scholar, but he was the well-rounded product of a sophisticated society. The man who was expert at horseshoes, could crack a walnut between thumb and forefinger, and was one of America's greatest horsemen was also a connoisseur of drama in Williamsburg and Philadelphia who particularly delighted in Joseph Addison's *Cato* and sprinkled his correspondence with references to Seneca and other classical writers.

Young George, who at age eleven lost his father, did not receive the English education provided for his two older brothers. He may have received some tutoring beyond the "old field school" from an Anglican minister in Fredericksburg. But whether he did or not, he received cultural advantages beyond most of his contemporaries. Both the Washingtons and the Balls, his mother's family, were prominent in the Northern Neck, the peninsula between the Rappahannock and Potomac rivers which was known as "the Athens of Virginia." His older half-brother Lawrence, one of the best-educated and most promising young men in Virginia, was a strong cultural influence. So were Lawrence's brother-in-law, a classically educated Englishman, William Fairfax, and William's wife, the charming and sophisticated Sally, who were neighbors. Significant too was the influence of another Fairfax, Washington's first employer, Thomas, sixth Baron Fairfax, an Oxford graduate and former contributor to *The Spectator*, Addison and Steele's great magazine. A self-taught architect who transformed a modest dwelling into the beautiful Mount Vernon, a knowledgeable collector and commissioner of significant paintings, and a lover of music, Washington was even more zealous in the pursuit of facts. Before Washington was a national leader, his participation in the Continental Congress of 1774 elicited from Patrick Henry an impressive compliment: "If you speak of solid information and sound judgement,

Colonel Washington is unquestionably the greatest man on that floor."

It is interesting that Henry praised Washington's store of "solid information." Washington was not much given to the discussion of abstractions except such cardinal concepts of his society as "honor," a compound of integrity and reputation. Nor was he, as an ultimately firm but reluctant revolutionist, inclined to needless discussion of ideas that provoked conflict among friends. It is therefore difficult to speak with assurance about many aspects of his religious belief.

Richard Brookhiser, in his *Founding Father: Rediscovering George Washington*, wrote, "No aspect of his life has been more distorted than his religion." But Brookhiser presents some clues and reaches at least one striking conclusion: "Besides the literature of American political theory, Washington was influenced by two coherent systems of thought—Christianity and Freemasonry."

Brookhiser notes that the first president, following his inauguration, walked to a church service at St. Paul's Chapel on Broadway but "seems not to have taken communion." The first lady, he notes, "invariably did." Contemporary sources mention other occasions on which Washington abstained from communion. One wonders why. Whatever the reason, it must have been a matter of conscience. A less scrupulous political leader would have taken refuge in conformity to have presented an appealing image to his constituents. Certainly he was not averse to worship.

The phraseology of Washington's farewell address owes more to James Madison and Alexander Hamilton than to the first president himself. But Washington insisted that their writing express his own convictions. The man who would not participate in communion simply to win public favor would not at the conclusion of his political career have endorsed popular views merely to win public approval. He declared in this final message as president: "Of all the dispositions and habits which lead to political prosperity, religion and morality are indispensable supports. In vain would that man claim the tribute of patriotism, who should labor to subvert these great pillars of human happiness, these finest props of the duties of men and citizens. The mere politician, equally with the pious man, ought to respect and cherish them."

Washington has been called a "warm Deist," meaning that while he believed the universe was governed by laws, he also believed that its Maker, far from remaining aloof from his creation, sometimes intervened directly in its affairs. In 1775, following Braddock's defeat and the experience of remaining unharmed when several bullets pierced his coat, Washington exclaimed in a personal letter: "See the wondrous works of Providence!" He was a twenty-three-year-old junior officer when he wrote that, but his attitude was the same after the Battle of Monmouth when the forty-six-year-old General Washington, in a letter to his brother, expressed gratitude to "that bountiful Providence which has never failed us in the hours of distress." His public statement as the victor at Yorktown in 1781 was consistent with these private comments. He called for worship in appreciation of the "reiterated and astonishing interpositions of Providence."

After these declarations of belief, especially the two addressed to individual correspondents, one his own brother, only a cynic would question Washington's sincerity in his first inaugural address when he spoke of the "providential agency" that had made the United States possible. Any suspicion that he may have been using the word "providential" as a careless synonym for "fortunate" is dispelled by his immediate assertion that such "reflections have forced themselves too strongly on [his] mind to be suppressed." Writing to Edmund Randolph while pondering whether to accept a second term as president, he said, "As the allwise disposer of events has hitherto watched over my steps, I trust that in the important one I may soon be called upon to take, he will mark the course so plainly . . . that [I] cannot mistake the way."

Washington was sometimes so lengthy in his testimonials to Providence that he once concluded such an expression in a personal letter with the words: "It will be time enough for me to turn preacher when my present appointment ceases, and therefore I shall add no more on the Doctrine of Providence."

Some have suggested that Washington's moral conduct owed more to the Stoic philosophers so often quoted by Enlightenment leaders than to any direct influence of Biblical doctrine. But the influence of Bible wording as well as Bible ideas is evident in some of his more notable writings. Like an earlier Virginia planter-statesman, Colonel William Byrd, he was wont to refer to life on his acres as an idyll "under my own vine and fig tree." On August 17, 1790, Washington used the phrase with peculiar appropriateness in a letter of moving eloquence to the Hebrew Congregation of Newport. As Jews they were inheritors of the traditions of Solomon, as indeed, once removed, were Christians. Finding inspiration in his favorite imagery from the First Book of Kings, Washington said:

> It is now no more that toleration is spoken of as if it was by the indulgence of one class of people that another enjoyed the exercise of their inherent natural rights. For happily the government of the United States, which gives to bigotry no sanction, to persecution no assistance, requires only that they who live under its protection should demean themselves as good citizens, in giving it on all occasions their effectual support. . . . May the children of the stock of Abraham, who dwell in this land, continue to merit and enjoy the good will of the other inhabitants while every one shall sit in safety under his own vine and fig tree and there shall be none to make him afraid.

Washington's letter seems to have been truly representative of his attitude. His conduct as president seems to have been free of religious bigotry.

Paul F. Boller, Jr., deserves credit for making a strong case in his *George Washington and Religion* that "Washington was no less firmly committed to religious liberty and freedom of conscience than were Thomas Jefferson and James Madison." He marshals many letters from Washington to support his thesis that the first president, in his opposition to bigotry, was an influential model for the nation he led.

In a letter of September 14, 1775, to Benedict Arnold, then a colonel preparing to invade a predominantly Catholic area of Canada, Washington wrote, "While we are contending for our own liberty, we should be very cautious of violating the rights of conscience in others, ever considering that God alone is the Judge of the Hearts of Men, and to him only in this case they are answerable."

On November 5, 1775, writing both as a pragmatic commander and a consistent advocate of religious liberty, he issued a general order forbidding the celebration among the troops of Pope's Day, an observance particularly popular among the militant Protestants of New England:

As the Commander in Chief has been apprized of a design formed for the observance of that ridiculous and childish custom of burning the effigy of the pope, he cannot help expressing his surprise that there should be officers and soldiers in this army so void of common sense as not to see the impropriety of such a step at this juncture, at a time when we are soliciting . . . the friendship and alliance of the people of Canada, whom we ought to consider as brethren embarked in the same cause; the defense of the general liberty of America. At such a juncture and in such circumstances, to be insulting their religion is not to be suffered or excused.

While Washington's church attendance for most of his life was usually in some Protestant sanctuary, most often of his own Episcopal denomination, he sometimes worshiped with Catholic congregations.

At another important time in his life, Washington had combined an echo from the Old Testament with a concept from the New. In 1783 in a circular to the governors of the thirteen states of the Union as he prepared to resign as commander of the Continental Army, he voiced an "earnest prayer" that his countrymen would "do justice" and "love mercy," words derived from Micah's question, "What doth the Lord require of thee, but to do justly, and to love mercy, and to walk humbly with thy God?" Coupled with this hope in his prayer was the wish that Americans would "demean ourselves with that charity, humility and pacific temper of mind which were the characteristics of the Divine Author of our blessed religion, and without an humble imitation of whose example in these things, we can never hope to be a happy nation." The reference to the "humility" of the "Divine Author" makes it clear that Jesus rather than the supreme Creator is referred to. The fact that Jesus is described as "Divine" seems to indicate that Washington viewed him as more than mortal.

What of Brookhiser's assertion that Washington was "influenced by two coherent systems of thought—Christianity and Freemasonry"? The biographer makes a good case for Washington's interest in Freemasonry. His activities as a mason are well documented. Doubtless the comfort that he found in the rituals of masonry was akin to that he found in the Episcopal Church. As for the principles of masonry, those that seemed to reflect Christian tenets obviously were the most important to him. The influence of Freemasonry per se was not comparable in magnitude to that of Christianity.

There is evidence of religious conviction in the way in which Washington met the challenges of life. What can we learn about his religion from the way he met the crisis of death?

Washington was near death twice in his presidency—in 1789 and 1790. On the first of these occasions, he told his physician, Dr. Samuel Bard, "I am not afraid to die, and therefore can hear the worst." On the second occasion, his demeanor was such that his wife said, "He seemed less concerned himself as to the event than perhaps any other person in the United States." He faced the prospect of death with what might be described as Christian fortitude. But others have called it Stoic courage—and that is Stoic with a capital S. They see Washington as steeped in the philosophy of Seneca and others of his school, sustained as much by pride before his own and successive generations as by humble acceptance of the fate assigned by his God. Presumably, in the face of death, he turned to the "comforts of religion and philosophy" that he had recommended to so many other people. But in what proportion? Was religion or philosophy the larger element in the compound? Perhaps they were inseparable. Like some medieval fathers of the church, Washington seemed to take from the classical philosophers those things which supported Christian conclusions.

Washington's death followed by little more than six years his admonition to his dying nephew to "submit with patience and resignation to the will of the Creator." This statement had been consistent with his previous utterances. It also was consistent with the way in which he faced his own demise.

On December 12, 1799, for a period of about five hours that brought rain, snow, and hail, Washington rode about his fields in a raw wind. He sat down to dinner without bothering to exchange his soaking wet clothes for dry ones. By the next morning he had a sore throat but did not let it stop him from again venturing out into wet weather, this time to mark trees for cutting. Later in the day, though he was quite hoarse, he refused medication. He had many times before treated the threat of illness casually and gotten by with it.

This time he did not get by. By the third day he was in considerable pain and fighting for his breath. In accordance with standard medical practice of the time, he was bled three times within twelve hours. The loss of blood further weakened him. Diagnosticians in our day believe that he died of acute epiglottitis caused by influenza or a flu-like bacterial infection.

For almost twenty hours, he died by painful inches, in the course of his suffering asking his physician to abandon efforts to save him, letting him "go off quietly." He was concerned for his wife's safety, apologized for being trouble to the man who was moving him, and repeatedly urged the faithful body servant standing at bedside to sit down. His secretary, Tobias Lear, said, "He died as he lived."

When he was near death, he experienced a reaction that sometimes causes the victim of a respiratory illness to feel better at such a time. Ever methodical, he felt his own pulse and then settled back, apparently in resignation. Minutes later, he was dead.

W. W. Abbot, Peter Henriques, and others have commented on the fact that on his deathbed Washington showed concern for the preservation of papers that would provide evidence of his character and rightful position in history. This concern need not suggest that the dying man had no faith in immortality beyond the human sphere. But he had always been ambitious, though not ruthlessly so. The desire for earthly immortality would be intensified in such a man if he were dying without leaving behind a single living descendant.

His ways of living and dying would have earned the respect of the Stoics. They also would garner the admiration of most Christians. Only one thing in his behavior would have troubled seriously other adherents of the faith that he professed. This was the fact that he often declined communion, perhaps always did.

Could it be that Washington was influenced by St. Paul's admonition in First Corinthians 11:25–29? In reference to Christ's last supper with his apostles, Paul wrote:

He took the cup, when he had supped, saying, This cup is the new testament in my blood; this do ye as oft as ye drink it, in remembrance of me.

For as often as ye eat this bread, and drink this cup, ye do shew the Lord's death till he come.

Wherefore whoever shall eat this bread and drink this cup of the Lord, unworthily; shall be guilty of the body and blood of the Lord.

But let a man examine himself, and so let him eat of that bread and drink of that cup.

For he that eateth and drinketh unworthily, eateth and drinketh damnation to himself.

Did Washington refrain from taking communion because of the warning in this passage? Did he question his own worthiness, not because of some hidden sin of great magnitude but because of his strict standard of self-judgment? Did he deplore his own lack of humility or his honest but energetic pursuit of riches? He always demanded a tremendous amount of himself.

Washington read Paul's words in the King James version of the Bible, with their promise of damnation to those who took communion "unworthily." If he had had access to some of the translations of a later day, with their warning against eating or drinking the sacrament "in an unworthy manner," that is, without proper reverence, he might have become a communicant. The modern translations are not so dauntingly minatory as the one with which he was familiar. But if he had not been accustomed to reading the King James version, his own prose would have lacked the grandeur that it sometimes attained when echoing that great masterpiece.

7

John Marshall

Argument grew hot one night among young men gathered in McGuire's Hotel in Winchester, Virginia. The subject of contention was not the likeliest candidate for political office, the fastest horse in the county, or the fairest young lady in the valley. It was the validity of Christian faith. The argument began at five o'clock and was still in progress when the clock struck eleven, and one of the participants turned to an elderly man seated in silence. "Well, my old gentleman," he said, more than a trifle superciliously, "what think you of these things?"

The old man's presence had been largely unnoticed as the evening wore on. On his arrival, some had noted the dilapidated state of his gig, its broken shafts held together by the twisted bark of a sapling. Its owner was tall, long-limbed, and large-boned, but his careless attire, including unfastened knee buckles allowing his knee breeches to droop, suggested a dilapidation matching that of his vehicle.

To the surprise of everyone present, the old man responded with alacrity, reciting the arguments that had been used against Christian doctrines and answering them with a devastating combination of learning and logic. The lounging stranger was transformed into a magisterial figure of commanding eloquence. He spoke for an hour. When he concluded, no one else spoke a word. Well he might seem magisterial; he was Chief Justice John Marshall.

The story of the debate in the hotel was carried by a local newspaper, the *Winchester Republican*, and was reprinted by other publications. There is no proof of its truth. Many have suspected it to be inaccurate, largely because of the propensity of some defenders of the faith to support their conviction with manufactured anecdotes suggesting the allegiance of respected historical figures. Marshall's most famous biographer, Albert J. Beveridge, in his monumental *Life of John Marshall*, includes the account but does not vouch for its truth.

Maybe no one will ever prove it accurate. But it does fit quite well the image of Marshall presented in some other stories whose truth is generally accepted. For instance, there is the tale of the young dandy who purchased a live turkey in a Richmond market, and anxious not to soil his elegant attire, asked a shabbily dressed old man to carry it home for him. When the young man tried in vain to tip the obliging old fellow, he was told that Mr. Marshall had a federal job that paid him quite well.

On another occasion, a young boy, unaware that the man he had met was the great chief justice, said, "He's a nice old man but he ain't got much sense."

When a farmer told one of his laborers that the gentleman the man had rescued from a driving mishap was "the great Chief Justice, the biggest lawyer in the United States," the worker replied,

"He may be the biggest lawyer in the United States, but he ain't got sense enough to back a gig off a sapling."

There are many verified tales of Marshall's unimpressive dress and demeanor, which lulled people into underestimating him, only to be amazed when some question engaged his heart and mind so that he fixed their attention with his magnetic gaze and overwhelmed them with a torrent of eloquent logic.

Marshall regularly attended Anglican services. Many writers have assumed that his faithfulness was influenced not so much by personal conviction as by a desire to encourage the attendance of those whose conduct would otherwise deteriorate. Still other writers have suggested that he attended church in deference to his wife, Mary, the "Dearest Polly" of his intimate correspondence. Beveridge implies that the chief justice was moved by both considerations. Certainly Marshall believed strongly that public officials should set good examples of conduct for their constituents. And certainly he was most uxorious in his tender care of his nervous and perpetually worried wife, who was often incapable of directing the servants in her home. Richmond friends arriving unexpectedly at the Marshall house were sometimes surprised to see the chief justice, a man of exalted position and notorious ineptitude in practical physical tasks, performing in a most unlikely guise: In rolled-up shirt sleeves and wearing a bandana on his head, he would be demonstrating to the household staff the necessary arts of scrubbing floors and of dusting walls as well as furniture.

But are these two motivations alone sufficient to explain regular worship under conditions as difficult as some of those that plagued Marshall? Bishop William Meade, a prominent Episcopal ecclesiastic of Marshall's time and the source of much information on the period, recalled services in Coolspring Meeting House attended by the great jurist. "I can never forget," Meade wrote, "how he would prostrate his tall form before the rude low benches, without backs, . . . in the middle of his children and grandchildren and his old neighbors." At Monumental Church, which he attended when in Richmond, he was perhaps as uncomfortable as at Coolspring. In the city church, said Meade, "he was much incommoded by the narrowness of the pews. . . . Not finding room enough for his whole body within the pew, he used to take his seat nearest the door of the pew, and throwing it open, let his legs stretch a little into the aisle."

Adding to the impression that Marshall was not a devoted worshiper, or in any event not a devout Christian, is the fact that he did not take communion. Beveridge says of the jurist, "He was a Unitarian in belief and therefore never became a member of the Episcopal church, to which his parents, wife, children, and all other relatives belonged." But George Washington, as was surely known by Marshall, his personal friend and copious biographer, was also a noncommunicant. Yet Marshall wrote of Washington, "Without making ostentatious professions of religion, he was a sincere believer in the Christian faith and a truly devout man."

We must conclude that Marshall thought it unreasonable to infer that a man was not a Christian simply because, for undisclosed reasons, he chose not to become a communicant. Some of the speculation about Washington's refraining from communion, presented in chapter 6, may apply equally to the chief justice.

Of course, we do not know how either Washington or Marshall defined "Christian." Neither is known to have been as explicit on the subject as Jefferson was in some private writings.

As for Christian ethics, Marshall certainly demonstrated them in a long life of private and public virtue. From youth onward, he earned a reputation for dependable integrity. His only questionable conduct as chief justice, while seemingly flagrant, was motivated by a sensitivity to others' feelings. During the treason trial of Aaron Burr, Marshall was a guest at a party attended by the defendant. When he accepted the invitation, the jurist did not know that the man appearing before him daily as a defendant was also invited. Out of concern for his host's feelings, Marshall unwisely remained at the same table with the accused.

Bishop Meade, himself a man of high principles, tells how Marshall excelled him in this regard. Riding together on a journey, they came to a stretch of road that was more an obstacle than a passage.

Seeing that a traveler had removed a section of fence to gain passage over someone's private acreage, the minister prepared to pursue the same path. But Marshall would not. Meade reported, "He said we had better go around, although each step was a plunge, adding that it was his duty, as one in office, to be very particular in regard to such things."

Typical of Marshall's secret charities was his gift to an old Revolutionary comrade that he chanced upon on the road from Richmond to Fauquier County. Marshall learned that the man was going to lose all his property because of a heavy burden of debt. They spent the night at the same inn. Marshall rose before his fellow veteran and left for him a check covering the entire debt. The man was grateful but unwilling to accept such a sacrifice. He rode after the jurist, overtook him, and returned the check. The beneficiary accepted the check only after Marshall agreed to take a lien on the land. As Marshall never foreclosed, his sacrifice prevailed.

He was far ahead of his time in insisting that women were "the friends, the companions, and the equals of man." Harriet Martineau, a prominent feminist, said that Marshall "maintained through life, and carried to his grave, a reverence for women as rare in its kind as in its degree." He once wrote, "I have always believed that national character as well as happiness depends more on the female part of society than is generally imagined."

In war and peace, in public and private life, Marshall exemplified Christian ethics. Apparently only in his long-cherished animosity for his cousin Thomas Jefferson, a fully reciprocated feeling, is he known to have violated Christ's admonition to forgive one's enemies.

But is the faithful following of the command to "do unto others as you would have them do unto you" sufficient to make one a Christian without faith in, and allegiance to, a divine Christ? Some of Marshall's contemporaries would have said yes. Others would have disagreed. And how can we know whether there were private declarations of faith by Marshall?

There is a report that, according to his daughter in her last illness, Marshall was converted to traditional Christian faith by reading *Keith on Prophecy*. She was quoted as saying that her father decided to "apply for permission to the communion of our church . . . but died without ever communing." The entire story may be true, but substantial proof is lacking. Many who appraise it are wary of the tendency of proselytizers to accept without question anything tending to bolster their own belief.

Marshall was certainly ethical and probably religious, but the exact tenets of his faith are unknown. There is no indication that he was determinedly hiding some great secret from the public. Despite his openhanded generosity and open-minded acceptance of most people's idiosyncracies, Marshall was reticent in private matters. The only thing we know about his attitude toward public worship is that he thought the population of the United States was more decent because of it. And he consciously supported the prestige of the Christian church by faithful attendance of its services.

8

Patrick Henry

T HE courthouse was packed with people who had braved the December cold and the rough roads of pre-Revolutionary Virginia's Hanover County. Some were dressed in the lace cuffs and colorful suits favored by many of the planter gentry. A much larger group wore the coarse cloth or leather garments that were a cleaner version of their laboring clothes. A small group seated together were dressed in the sober black of the Anglican clergy. Even more than their garb, their relaxed and smiling countenances set them apart from the mostly anxious-faced audience.

The parsons had reason to be pleased. As ministers of the Established Church, they had successfully carried to the Privy Council in

London a protest against the Virginia legislature's practice of ordering Anglican priests' pay from the government to be in tobacco or in more traditional currency, according to which would be less costly to the taxpayers. This victory had inspired the ministers to sue for back pay for the period in which they had been paid by the less remunerative system.

The class action was initiated through suit in the Hanover court by Rev. James Maury, an Anglican priest from the adjacent county of Louisa. He basked in the congratulations of his colleagues. After the Privy Council's action, prospects were bright that compensation would be awarded for salary lost under the now disallowed system.

Any possibility of successfully opposing the clerics' demand seemed swept away when the opposition's attorney, the well-regarded John Lewis, withdrew from the case and was replaced by the only local attorney who seemed willing to accept it. He was a twenty-seven-year-old lawyer of little legal experience, a twice-failed storekeeper who had married at eighteen and since had been barely able to support his rapidly growing family. The clergymen are said to have smiled at the discomfiture of the many plain people who did not wish them well. When the young lawyer arose, gangling and awkward, and with much hesitation began his plea, the parsons were delighted that the case for their opponents was dependent on this man, young Patrick Henry.

But suddenly the speaker's voice became resonant and confident. His gestures were forceful and sweeping. Struck by the transformation, most of his hearers thrilled to his words. With slight variations in wording, many would long remember one sentence that he spoke: "Such is the avarice, such the insatiate thirst for gold of these ecclesiastical harpies, that they would snatch the last hoe cake from the widow and the orphan."

Under the law, the jury had no choice but to award damages to the suing clergy. But the jurymen showed their contempt for the reverend petitioners by limiting damages to one penny. The mass of plain people in attendance were wild with enthusiasm. They had found a powerful voice. Even the presiding justice, though an Anglican vestryman and sometime churchwarden, was moved to "tears of ecstacy."

At a later date, Edmund Randolph, himself an accomplished orator, wrote, "After every illusion had vanished, a prodigy yet remained. It was Patrick Henry, born in obscurity, poor, and without the advantages of literature, rousing the genius of his country." Without intending to, Randolph, usually a dependable chronicler of historic events as well as a leading participant, lent his prestige to the creation of a Henry legend.

Obviously, he in no way exaggerated the great orator's eloquence, but he was misinformed about Henry's origins. One might wonder why the presiding justice of Hanover County, being so prominent in the affairs of the Established Church, did not recuse himself from this case. The eighteenth century was not as particular in such matters as its successors. Besides, it may have been assumed that any bias he had in favor of the Anglican clergyman was offset by the fact that the opposing attorney was his own son.

In a day of growing populism, especially in the back country, Henry, who had political ambitions, found it valuable to stress an affinity with plain people. The truth of the matter is that many people would consider the circumstances of the young orator's origin and nurture decidedly advantageous. John Henry, his father, besides being Hanover County's presiding justice and a prominent Anglican layman, was also the commanding colonel of the county militia. Of all of the parents of America's Founding Fathers, Colonel Henry had the most distinguished formal education. He was a graduate of the rigorous classical curriculum of Scotland's famous Aberdeen University. For five years, he was Patrick's tutor, drilling him in Greek and Latin literature.

Patrick's parents had an estate of more than 2,500 acres. Colonel William Byrd II of Westover, a sophisticated planter-scholar often called the most polished gentleman in America, said that Patrick's mother was one of the most accomplished female conversationalists in Virginia. The parents' record of accomplishment was not unique in the family. Of the twelve men who governed Hanover County and conducted its courts, six (counting Colonel Henry) were their kinsmen.

So Edmund Randolph, who was right about so many things, was wrong in his assumption that Patrick Henry was "born in obscurity, poor, and without the advantages of literature." He was entirely correct in pronouncing the man a prodigy.

The oratorical prowess that Henry demonstrated first in the little courtroom in Hanover would carry his name to Europe in his lifetime and ultimately to every civilized country in the world. Nearly always, when he was admired, he would be celebrated as a true man of the people and cited as evidence of the ability of rugged worth to triumph over artificial advantages. Lord Byron saluted him as the "forest-born Demosthenes," a designation whose significance would not have been lost on the back-country lawyer tutored by his classically trained father.

In the aftermath of his defeat, the Rev. Mr. Maury wrote: "After the court adjourned, [Henry] apologized to me for what he had said, alleging that his sole view in engaging in the cause, and in saying what he had, was to render himself popular. You see, then, it is so clear a point in this person's opinion that the ready road to popularity here is to trample under foot the interests of religion, the rights of the church, and the prerogatives of the Crown."

Henry's triumph, after repeated failures in several occupations, failures made more conspicuous by the success of his father and other relatives, was a heady experience for the young man. He was on his way to becoming a demagogue. Whether he would remain one would be a matter for speculation.

Henry was not ignorant of sacred writings. As Robert Douthat Meade pointed out in his excellent *Patrick Henry: Patriot in the Making*, the orator made effective use of Biblical phrases and analogies. Some of these he may have picked up from church services and from conversations with his uncle, the Rev. Patrick Henry, an Anglican minister. But it is likely that some of it was from Bible reading on his own. Whether he undertook this activity in search of spiritual wisdom or solely from delight in the text's sonorous tones and majestic rhythms cannot be known.

In 1765, two years after the Parsons' Cause, Henry was a freshman member of the House of Burgesses, the lower chamber of Virginia's bicameral legislature. He had served only a week when a historic event occurred—one which caused him to ignore the time-honored advice to novice legislators to be seen but not heard.

As a result of his oratorical performance in the Parsons' Cause, a reputation as a foe of religion had preceded him to the capital in Williamsburg. But in friendly conversation with fellow burgesses, he often allayed hostility. Members variously found him "amiable," were impressed with the "mildness of his temper," and even conjectured that he had "imbibed a disposition to religion and virtue."

After Patrick Henry had served his first week as a fledgling legislator, there arrived in Williamsburg the news that Parliament in London had adopted a resolution preparatory to imposing a new tax on the colonies. Under the proposed Stamp Act, stamps would be required for every kind of legal paper—bills of lading, bills of sale, contracts—and for newspapers, individual advertisements in newspapers, pamphlets, almanacs, calendars, packs of cards, land survey orders, college diplomas, and "every skin or piece of vellum or parchment, or sheet on which shall be engrossed or printed a declaration."

Coincident with Henry's entrance upon his legislative career, a bloc of members from the highland counties, dissatisfied with the leadership of Tidewater river barons, were searching for a leader round whom they could rally.

On May 26, 1765, a burgess rose to move that the House go into Committee of the Whole to consider "steps necessary to be taken in consequence of the Resolutions of the House of Commons of Great Britain relative to the charging of certain stamp duties in the Colonies and Plantations of America." Patrick Henry seconded the motion. Soon the dissident members would know that they had found their leader.

In the committee session of the whole House, Henry presented a series of resolutions. The first declared that "the first adventurers and settlers" of Virginia "brought with them and transmitted to their posterity and all other [of] his Majesty's subjects inhabiting" the colony "all the privileges, franchises, and immunities that have at any time been held, enjoyed, and possessed by the people of Great Britain."

The culminating resolution stated that the General Assembly of Virginia had the "exclusive right and power to lay taxes and impositions upon the inhabitants of this colony, and that every attempt to vest such power in any person or persons whatsoever, other than the General Assembly . . . has a manifest tendency to destroy British as well as American freedom."

As the burgesses voted separately on individual resolutions comprising the whole, each of the first four passed, but none by a margin of more than three votes. The fifth was the crucial one, the boldest of all, the one asserting that only Virginia's representatives had the right to tax Virginians. Prospects for its passage seemed dim.

At this point, Henry took the floor. Gaunt and plain-garbed, like a figure in a morality play, he swept the house with a lightning glance and hurled his words like avenging bolts. Self-taxation, he thundered, was essential to freedom. As his voice now rose to a roar, now sank to a whisper, it was almost like a multitude of immortal voices rushing down the winds of time. Here and there a listener sat taller in his seat as he saw himself an actor in a universal drama.

The excitement was already almost unbearable when Henry shouted that the Stamp Act was tyrannical and then, with mounting emphasis, cried out:

"Caesar had his Brutus, Charles the First his Cromwell, and George the Third—"

"Treason!" shouted the Speaker of the House.

"And George the Third," finished Henry, "may he never have either."

The nine concluding words may seem less dramatic than those

frequently attributed to the orator: "And George the Third, may he profit from their example. If this be treason, make the most of it." Apparently the more cautious version is likely to be accurate. It was certainly a shrewder reply. It implied that King George was following in the footsteps of tyrants but was phrased in a way that suggested concern for the sovereign's safety.

Henry's statement was sufficiently potent. The resolution carried by a single vote. Later the dominant conservatives had the most offensive words expunged from the record. But the resolves as originally worded circulated through the thirteen colonies. The chronically failing young man of two years ago was a famous success.

The royal governor, Lord Dunmore, dissolved the colonial assembly. Under Henry's leadership, they gathered at a nearby tavern and issued the call for a continental congress.

In 1775, Henry called for armed resistance to Britain's colonial policy. He gave the Revolutionary cause its rallying cry and provided one of the world's most famous quotations when he exclaimed, "Give me liberty or give me death!" Henry and Jefferson had once been friends, but even at a later date, when they were no longer friends, Jefferson said that the radical leader was "the greatest orator who ever lived." Henry became a member of the Continental Congress. There he was celebrated above all others for his eloquence. In our time, few of the nation's Founding Fathers enjoy as large an international reputation.

His fellow Virginians loved no one more. He served as governor, turned down national offices that he was begged to accept, notably secretary of state and chief justice of the United States, and returned to Virginia's legislature. There his eloquence carried the day for measures that otherwise would have had little chance. An adverse speech by him could kill an initially popular bill. Eventually he could deter the introduction of bills he disliked by merely threatening to make speeches against them.

With the end of the Revolution, Henry found himself in disagreement with many of his fellow Founding Fathers. He had often seemed the most radical of the lot with the possible exception of Samuel Adams of Massachusetts. Henry was among the first to call for American independence, pressing for it at a time when some future leaders of the Revolution were still urging moderation. But whereas the winning of American independence was his final goal, such compatriots as Jefferson and Madison celebrated it as an opportunity for major reforms in government. And John Adams said the real revolution would occur not on the battlefields but in the minds of men.

Henry was the first governor of Virginia as a commonwealth rather than a colony. But he was not happy in the executive role. The Virginia constitution, written by men who had known the pain of gubernatorial tyranny, was designed to make the governor little more than a figurehead. The mazes of prescribed procedure were as confining as the maze of hedges in the formal gardens outside the windows of the governor's palace.

As a legislator, state or national, Henry found liberation. His passionate eloquence was a more effective tool than constitutional prescriptions. But he did not believe that stronger government, especially national government, was the answer to besetting problems. When the Constitution of the United States was submitted to ratifying conventions in the individual states, all eyes were turned toward Virginia. If that powerful state proved a wedge rather than a link between states to the north and south, there could be no effective American union. Henry feared domination by a strong republic as much as he did the tyranny of an empire. In the Virginia Convention to consider ratification, his was the most powerful voice of opposition.

If he had succeeded in thwarting the founding of the American republic, Henry would have changed history in a way that virtually all American historians today, and a great many of their counterparts in other nations, would consider a tremendous loss to freedom in the world.

But since even Henry's great eloquence threatened but did not triumph, the Constitution was the better for it. To allay fears raised by the orator, the proponents of ratification had to agree to add by amendment a bill of rights including a pledge of religious freedom.

By this time, it was obvious that Henry was no longer a radical. He became a Federalist, a supporter of the more conservative of the two parties that dominated American government in the early years. And this fact revealed something about his own development. The man who loved his country but had long been in danger of becoming a demagogue was now willing to stand boldly for his convictions, even when they were unpopular with the mass of his countrymen.

Before ratification of the Constitution of the United States in 1788, the failed farmer and storekeeper had become a rich attorney. The master of 22,000 acres, he was the fourteenth largest landholder in Virginia. But he was no mere materialist. Some of his associates thought that he was obsessed with the idea that the survival of republican government depended upon private as well as public virtue.

He was no longer the bane of the Episcopal clergy in Virginia but their most influential supporter. Earlier in his career, he had defended Baptist preachers who were fined or imprisoned for preaching without a license, this license being unobtainable unless they forsook their denominational faith. There is evidence that, in so doing, Henry was seeking neither popularity nor remuneration. When he secured the release from jail of a Rev. John Weatherford, a Baptist minister, only to discover that the clergyman could not be freed without the payment of a sum beyond the man's means, Henry paid the considerable bill himself and concealed that fact. Not until many years later did Weatherford learn of his secret benefactor.

In his later years, however, Henry was Virginia's stoutest defender of the Episcopal Church, successor to the Anglican Church, as the established Church of Virginia. When the Virginia General Assembly enacted into law, effective in January 1786, Thomas Jefferson's eloquent Statute for Religious Freedom, it was over Henry's vigorous objections. In fact, Henry was so persuasive and resourceful in his efforts to preserve the Episcopal Church's Establishment status that Jefferson once wrote Madison that the best hope for religious liberty lay in praying that Henry would die before the next session of the legislature. Allowance must be made for Jefferson's facetiousness in addressing his best friend, but his frustration was sincere.

Perceiving that there was no great eagerness among other denominations to preserve special advantages for the Episcopal Church, Henry proposed Establishment status for four denominations: Episcopalians, Presbyterians, Methodists, and Baptists. This proposal was thwarted when the Baptists replied that, if official status for Episcopalians was unfair, so was such an advantage for Baptists or any other denomination. The Presbyterians and Methodists followed suit. Despite Henry's efforts, church and state were separated in Virginia.

In his last years, Henry was appalled by the excesses of the French Revolution. Not only were the executions shocking but so was the official French enmity to religion. He feared that France would pull down "the great pillars of all government and of social life." These, he said, were "virtue, morality, and religion." Judge Spencer Roane, his son-in-law, noted that the old man was becoming "more religious." He tried to convert some of his associates to Christianity, read the Bible each morning, was disturbed to learn that some people supposed him a Deist, and declared that Deism was "another name for vice and depravity."

His agitation was quieted by reflections that, "from its first appearance in the world," Christianity had "been attacked in vain by all the wits, philosophers, and wise ones aided by every power of man, and its triumph has been complete." Of the anti-Christian forces, he said, "the puny efforts of [Thomas] Paine are thrown in to prop their tottering fabric, whose foundations cannot stand the test of time."

One of those whom Henry strove to convince of the blessings of Christianity was his physician and friend Dr. George Cabell. The doctor was with Henry when the old statesman died. At first, the orator sat silent, watching his nails turn blue as the blood retreated from his fingers. When he knew the end was imminent, Henry pulled a cap over his eyes and prayed for his family, his country, and his soul. He then asked the doctor to note the help of religion to one about to die. He said that his religion had never failed him.

Among the papers that Henry left for his executors were his will, his Stamp Act Resolutions of 1765 together with an explanation of his activities in connection with them, and a message to future generations of Americans. In it the great orator, who as a fiery young patriot had earned a reputation for hostility to religion, said of American independence: "Whether this will prove a blessing or a curse, will depend upon the use our people make of the blessings which a gracious God hath bestowed on us. If they are wise, they will be great and happy. If they are of a contrary character, they will be miserable. Righteousness alone can exalt them as a nation." One can almost see him lifting his head from his desktop labors, and with his glasses shoved up on his forehead in the familiar way, turning his penetrating gaze to posterity. The last sentence he wrote was:

"Reader! whoever thou art, remember this; and in Thy sphere, practice virtue thyself, and encourage it in others."

9

Alexander Hamilton

THE "bastard brat of a Scotch peddler." That is what John Adams called Alexander Hamilton. Thomas Jefferson's language was more elevated, but his condemnation of Hamilton was even more severe. In a letter to George Washington, the Virginian called the New Yorker "a man whose history from the moment at which history can stoop to notice him, is a tissue of machinations against the liberty of the country which has not only received [him] and given him bread, but heaped its honors on his head."

Hamilton, who prided himself on his logic, had crowned a vitriolic denunciation of Jefferson with his ultimate epithet, charging that the third president was "paradoxical." Many writers since, including some to whom the adjective was not nearly as censorious as it seemed to Hamilton, have followed him in applying the same term to the Sage of Monticello. Actually the label might be applied to Hamilton himself with equal appropriateness. Technically, Adams was correct in describing Hamilton as a "bastard." A court record in his native British West Indies described the infant Alexander as a "whore child." But the circumstances were not quite what the term implied. Before her fifteen-year union with Alexander's father, his mother had fled from a teenage marriage forced upon her by her own mother. Apparently subjected to ill treatment by her domineering spouse, who even had her imprisoned, she eventually fled from him and formed an alliance with James Hamilton, a merchant. Her husband divorced her, and the terms of the divorce prevented legal marriage to anyone else. The paradoxical element regarding Alexander Hamilton's birth is that, while he fretted over the stain of illegitimacy, he boasted that he had "better pretensions than most of those who in this country plume themselves on ancestry." And he said that government should be by "the wealthy and the well-born."

The reference to the wealthy introduces another element of paradox. Hamilton was famed for his hard-headed business sense and for his appreciation of the commercial aspects of government, yet he never attained personal wealth. Indeed, for some years when he proudly refused the financial aid of his wife's wealthy family, he was glad to accept the provender of their gardens as a way of reducing his grocery bills. The contrast between Hamilton's success in public finance and near failure in private was noted by the diplomat Talleyrand who, during his service in America, often saw a laboring Hamilton framed by one of the few lighted windows on his street. The Frenchman wrote, "I have seen a man who made the fortune of a nation, laboring all night to support his family."

What was the basis of Hamilton's boast about his ancestry? His mother was the daughter of a French Huguenot physician. The statesman's paternal line was more famous. His father was James

Hamilton XV, a merchant more notable for his forebears than for personal success. A Scotsman, he came from a long line of lairds, had sprung from the Ducal family of Hamilton, and was the grandson of Sir Robert Pollock, Baronet.

The combination of shame and pride engendered in Alexander Hamilton by his attitude toward his heritage made him extraordinarily sensitive and accounts for some of the frustrations he suffered throughout his life. The sensitivity was increased by the fact that, while still a child, he was deserted by his father, lost his mother to death, and became the ward of a maternal relative, who soon committed suicide.

Another paradoxical aspect of Hamilton involved his military career. At age seventeen, he had written, "I wish there was a war." All his life, he coveted military glory. In the Revolution, he pestered Washington, who found him indispensable at headquarters, until the general in the eleventh hour yielded to his pleas for a field command. This was at Yorktown, and he served with distinction. Though he filled high civil posts, including the office of secretary of the treasury in Washington's cabinet, he particularly cherished the title of colonel. When he and Jefferson served together in the cabinet, the revelation that the Virginian's great heroes were Bacon, Newton, and Locke prompted Hamilton to exclaim that Julius Caesar was the greatest man who ever lived. Many people concluded that Hamilton, though lacking moral courage, had enough animal courage to be careless of danger in the pursuit of glory. They had not heard that a grizzled veteran, eyeing Hamilton's shaking knees before his baptism of fire, had contemptuously asked,

"What's the matter, Mr. Hamilton, are you afraid?" And that Hamilton had replied, "Yes, I'm afraid, and if you were half as scared as I am you would run."

Oscar Wilde once told a customs inspector, "I have nothing to declare but my genius." When the teenage Alexander arrived on the mainland of North America in 1772, he could have made the same declaration. As a child, he was employed by an international wholesale import–export firm. By the time Alexander was sixteen or less, the manager made a transatlantic journey that necessitated an absence of several months. During this time, the boy not only bought and sold cargoes but also directed the activities of ship captains.

The apparently efficient performance of these duties did not claim all his attention. His reading ranged from Alexander Pope and Plutarch to volumes of math and chemistry. He was also writing poems and prose essays, publishing some, and in his native colony building a reputation for literary precocity. When that productive intellect had reached maturity, the brilliant Talleyrand said, "I consider Napoleon, [Charles James] Fox, and Hamilton the three greatest men of our epoch, and if I had to choose between [sic] the three, I would give, without hesitation, the first place to Hamilton."

There is ambivalence even about the date of Hamilton's birth. He himself said the correct date was January 11, 1757, but a legal document in the records of his native colony gives the year as 1755. The record, however, dates from more than a decade after the event. Some think that Hamilton was mistaken. Others suggest that he deliberately falsified the record so that two extra years of youth would make him seem more precocious. Most historians accept the earlier date, and I have joined them, though with less complete assurance.

Precocity carried the teenage Alexander to the North American mainland in 1774. The agent of destiny was a Presbyterian minister. The Rev. Hugh Knox, a Scotsman from Ulster, arrived in St. Croix in 1772 and was soon impressed with the youngster's brilliance in combination with industriousness and dependability. Knox was a physician and a teacher as well as a Presbyterian clergyman. He aspired to be one "who draws genius out of obscurity." Knox not only guided the youngster's studies but also pointed him toward piety. A so-called New Sides Presbyterian, the preacher belonged to the most radical wing of the Kirk of Scotland, one inclined to republican ideas. He instilled in Alexander a hatred of slavery and a desire to attend his own alma mater, Princeton. Soliciting the cooperation of philanthropic businessmen, he made it possible for his protégé to go to New Jersey to further his education.

To prepare him for entrance to Princeton, he was enrolled in the Elizabethan Academy. There the courses in mathematics, Latin, and Greek went far beyond anything he had known. Ordinarily, if the student was apt, the course upon which he entered required two to three years. Alexander completed the work in less than a year.

Then he asked Dr. John Witherspoon, the famous president of Princeton, to admit him to the university with the understanding that he would be promoted from class to class in each discipline according to his personal progress in each subject, quite independently of the prescribed terms. Witherspoon did not dismiss Alexander as a bumptious boy. Only after conferring with the trustees did he refuse. Alexander sought the same arrangement with Myles Cooper, president of King's College (now Columbia University), and obtained what he wanted.

Though carrying more than a full curriculum at the New York college, Hamilton was really majoring in revolution. Soon after his matriculation, the Boston Tea Party, a radical if not irresponsible act in the eyes of even such earnest patriots as John Adams and Benjamin Franklin, stirred the spirit of revolution throughout the colonies. During his freshman year, London's Coercive Acts and the convening of America's First Continental Congress brought the crisis nearer to war. The campus was seething with revolt, and Hamilton, a slender figure with reddish blond hair, looking much younger than most of his fellow students, was a stirring orator at mass meetings. President Cooper was far more conservative than the students, and he often must have regretted his decision to admit Hamilton under an unorthodox arrangement when he could easily have refused. According to one report, Cooper once saw a large number of excited students gathered outside his home. They were listening to Hamilton. The president immediately jumped to the conclusion that the ungrateful young cur was denouncing him, the very man who had departed from tradition to enable him to enter college on special terms. Actually, Hamilton, fair-minded though passionate, was pleading with his fellow students to desist from harassing the president, whom he described as "an honest man." At this point, Cooper, completely misunderstanding the situation, raised the window and yelled, "Don't believe him. Every word he speaks is a lie."

Soon Hamilton's views reached an audience far beyond the confines of the campus. He published three political pamphlets, *A Full Vindication of the Measures of the Congress*, *The Farmer Refuted*, and *Remarks on the Quebec Act*. Publication at first was anonymous. Such was the treatises' quality that initially commentators attributed the first to John Jay and the second to John Adams.

Hamilton prepared for the war on the battlefield as well as for the one in men's minds that John Adams talked about. The youngster's preparation was partly a matter of principle but also a reflection of the thirst for military glory that he had confessed before leaving St. Croix. With some of his classmates, he formed a volunteer company that practiced the manual of arms under the direction of a retired major. His baptism of fire came on an August night in 1775 when, in helping to remove cannon from the battery, he came under the guns of a British warship. Soon he was studying the science of artillery. In the winter, when he was twenty by one reckoning, only eighteen by another, he was commissioned captain of an artillery company. He commanded sixty-eight officers and men.

Rising to the rank of lieutenant colonel, Hamilton served as Washington's private secretary and aide-de-camp from 1777 to 1781. His close association with Washington, almost becoming a surrogate son to the childless commander, played a decisive role in his subsequent career.

The major facts of that career are an integral part of American history and too well known to require detailed treatment here. He practiced law in New York City and served in Congress and as a delegate from New York State to the Annapolis Convention of 1786, which was called to consider the commercial problems of states comprising the Union. As the most influential member of that convention, he drafted a report leading to the Constitutional Convention of 1787, which produced the Constitution of the United States. With James Madison and John Jay, he coauthored

The Federalist, a series of essays instrumental in ratification of the Constitution and an enduring masterpiece of political philosophy.

As secretary of the treasury, Hamilton was one of the most influential members of Washington's cabinet. His frequently successful advocacy of measures to strengthen the national government in relations with the states brought him into bitter conflict with Secretary of State Thomas Jefferson. The United States developed a two-party system, with the Federalists following Hamilton and the Republicans taking their cue from Jefferson.

In 1798, when some Federalists feared there would be a war with France, an army was raised under General Washington to repel invasion. Hamilton successfully sought a commission as major general and second in command. He exulted in the prominent military role but was frustrated when President Adams prevented him from invading Spanish territory in Louisiana and Florida and Congress forced the disbanding of the army.

Hamilton's approach to foreign policy was quite independent of religious influence. He believed that nations need not follow the moral precepts proposed for individual human conduct and may instead rely entirely on self-interest.

Hamilton had dreams of becoming governor of New York and president of the United States. But he antagonized President Adams, and when the chief executive sought a second term, composed a verbal attack on him and circulated it among prominent Federalists. But he swallowed his prejudice to support Adams in order to block Aaron Burr's attempts to lead the Federalists. Eventually he even supported his bitter rival Jefferson to defeat Burr's presidential ambitions. These complex enmities killed Hamilton's own chances for political advancement. The quarrel with Burr would terminate Hamilton's life as well as his career.

Even before Hamilton left Washington's cabinet, where he had performed so brilliantly and been so influential, his life was on a downward course and he was almost stifled by depression. Political frustration was not the only cause. Financial problems and his wife's lingering illness were strong contributing factors. Apparently, through all these vicissitudes, religion brought little comfort. In this period of misery, a still worse threat descended—a scandal that could wreck his domestic life and permanently stain his carefully cultivated reputation.

The trouble began in the summer of 1791, when he was still secretary of the treasury. Hamilton had remained behind in Philadelphia after dispatching his wife and children to her family's estate near Albany, supposedly a healthier location during the hot months. While he was living alone, a beautiful woman suddenly appeared on his doorstep. She introduced herself as Maria Reynolds and said that her husband, James, had deserted her and their five-year-old child. She had no funds for travel to her family. In her helplessness, she appealed for aid to Hamilton as a fellow New Yorker known for benevolence.

Hamilton apparently found it difficult to believe that any normal man could abandon such a magnificent woman, one who combined every sensory attraction with all the obvious refinement of a born lady. He said that he did not have funds with him but would get money to her if she would leave her address. That night he carried a thirty dollar banknote to her residence. She received him in an upstairs bedroom. As Hamilton later explained, "Some conversation ensued from which it was quickly apparent that other than pecuniary consolation would be acceptable." A series of assignations followed.

One day Maria told him that her husband had returned and proposed a reconciliation. Hamilton advised her to accept. Though still powerfully attracted to her, Hamilton may have welcomed a turn of events that rescued him from his own folly.

But he was not to escape so lightly. Soon she told him that her husband had information on improprieties in Hamilton's Treasury Department and wanted to make a public exposure. Hamilton asked Mr. Reynolds to disclose the facts to him. Reynolds said that he soon would reveal to Hamilton a way in which the secretary could be helpful. At this point, the statesman appears to have suspected that husband and wife might have collaborated in entrapping him. His suspicions were confirmed when he learned that Reynolds had a reputation for skulduggery.

When Reynolds announced that Hamilton had promised him a job in the Treasury Department, the secretary resolved to end the affair with Maria immediately. But passion weakened his resolve and he persuaded himself that the best course would be to break away gradually.

Later, when Reynolds charged Hamilton's department with dishonest operations, the only way the secretary could prove his integrity as a public official and preserve public confidence in the administration he served was to reveal the sordid affair.

More pain was in store for Hamilton within his own family. In 1801, his beloved son Philip, a twenty-year-old graduate of Columbia, was involved in a quarrel leading to a duel with a lawyer. According to Thomas W. Rathbone, one of Philip's classmates, Alexander Hamilton "commanded his son, when on the ground, to reserve his fire till after [his opponent] had shot and then to discharge his pistol in the air." This unusual instruction from a loving father was a compromise between Alexander Hamilton's moral opposition to dueling and his realization that any man who refused to present himself as a target when challenged was vulnerable to charges of cowardice.

Philip was mortally wounded in the duel. He lay in intense pain on his deathbed, his mother lying next to him on one side, his father on the other. More than four months later, Alexander Hamilton had recovered sufficiently to reply to letters of condolence.

Philip was Hamilton's firstborn and was said to be his favorite child. Upon his graduation, his father compiled a set of rules for him to live by. Among other things, he was instructed to attend church every Sunday and spend the rest of the day "in innocent recreation." His father ordered that he "must not depart from any of these rules without my permission."

Hamilton's prescription of formal religion for his favorite child signaled a change in his own attitude. In earlier years, he had seemed rather casual about religion except when he was writing

Washington's farewell address, and then the emphasis on faith was in accordance with the president's instructions. Even before Philip's death, Hamilton's frustration over other matters had caused him to seek consolation in religion. After Philip's death, his father turned increasingly to things of the spirit.

Replying to a note of sympathy from Dr. Benjamin Rush, the great Philadelphia physician and Republican patriot, Hamilton wrote, "My loss is indeed great. But why should I repine? It was the will of heaven, and he is now out of the reach of the seductions and calamities of a world full of folly, full of vice, full of danger."

Hamilton seemed to have lost his appetite for earthly contests. In February 1802, with Jefferson as the popular president, Hamilton wrote to Gouverneur Morris: "Perhaps no man in the United States has sacrificed or done more for the present Constitution than myself—and contrary to all my anticipations of its fate, . . . I am still laboring to prop the frail and worthless fabric. Yet I have the murmurs of its friends no less than the curses of its foes for my rewards. What can I do better than withdraw from the scene? Every day proves to me more and more that this American world was not for me."

Adding to his disappointment in the republic he had helped to build was the secessionist movement initiated in New England and supported by leading officeholders in those states and New York. The movement died, but for a while it threatened the Union.

However disappointed in his country, Hamilton could not after all remain aloof from its troubles. The solution he advocated was surprising even to some who had worked with him for years. In the spring of 1802, he proposed a national organization of Christian activists to work for a conservative political agenda. He suggested that it be named the Christian Constitutional Society. As outlined by Hamilton, the organization would be led by a president and a twelve-member national directing council. Leadership in each state would be reposed in a vice president and a twelve-member sub-council. Local societies in communities of the individual states would meet weekly to discuss Christian and constitutional aspects of current events. The chapters would work "in concert to promote the election of fit men." They would also do charitable work, assist immigrants, and operate schools.

Substantial refutation of the supposition that Hamilton's advocacy was merely a cynical bit of political strategy is provided by his children's recollections of his reading the Bible to them and leading them in prayer. Maybe adversity caused him to seek refuge in the loving God to whom he had been introduced many years earlier by his benefactor, the Rev. Hugh Knox.

What success Hamilton might have had with a Christian Constitutional Society must remain a matter of speculation. Events intervened to end his life abruptly in his late forties.

He and Aaron Burr had long been enemies. Though Burr's candidacy for governor of New York was favored by Hamilton's own Federalist Party, Hamilton himself endorsed the Republican opponent. Burr was defeated and was almost crazy with frustrated ambition. When he heard reports that Hamilton had said he had a "despicable opinion" of him, Burr challenged Hamilton to a duel.

The whole affair must have reminded Hamilton of his son Philip's fatal duel. He followed the advice that he had given Philip. Though he abhorred the custom of dueling, he believed that he could not decline the challenge without incurring charges of cowardice. He felt that his honor made such a retreat unacceptable. The two antagonists met on the heights of Weehawken, where Philip had suffered his mortal wound three years earlier.

In a note to his wife, Hamilton said, "The scruples of a Christian have determined me to expose my own life to any extent rather than subject myself to the guilt of taking the life of another. This much increases my hazards, and redoubles my pangs for you. But you had rather I should die innocent than live guilty. . . . Adieu, my darling, darling wife."

In line with this message, he followed the advice he had given his son, to fire into the air rather than at his opponent. Burr's bullet tore into Hamilton's abdomen. "This is a mortal wound, Doctor," Hamilton told the examining physician. He was right, but death did not come for more than thirty hours. On his deathbed, he attempted to comfort his wife, saying, "Remember, my Eliza, you are a Christian."

After the doctors confirmed Hamilton's own diagnosis that he was mortally wounded, the dying man sent for the Rt. Rev. Benjamin Moore, Episcopal bishop of New York and president of Columbia. Hamilton asked the bishop to administer holy communion. After talking with Hamilton, Moore said that he was not sure that, given the circumstances of the duel, he could conscientiously administer the sacrament. Without having resolved where his duty lay, the bishop left. Later, as Hamilton's life ebbed, someone in the house sent for Moore again. When the bishop appeared, Hamilton said, "My dear Sir, you perceive my unfortunate position and no doubt have been made acquainted with the circumstances which led to it." He renewed his request for communion.

As Moore explained his hesitancy, Hamilton said he understood. The bishop added that he was concerned about the consequences if Hamilton should unexpectedly recover. "Will you never be engaged in a similar transaction?" Moore asked. "And will you employ all your influence in society to discountenance the barbarous custom?"

"That, Sir," said Hamilton, "is my deliberate intention."

The bishop then asked, "Are you disposed to live in love and charity with all men?"

Raising his hands, the dying man answered, "I have no ill will against Colonel Burr. I met him with a fixed resolution to do him no harm. I forgive all that happened."

The bishop administered the sacrament.

The financial wizard celebrated on two continents died heavily in debt. But he was rich in friendship, and some of his friends paid the debts and made provision for his widow and his children.

Ever paradoxical, Hamilton, who had seemed to abandon his early piety for a more casual attitude to religion, had become intensely reverent. He had never had the opportunity to execute his plans for a national organization of Christians to elect like-minded men to political office, to establish schools, and to circulate Christian-oriented publications commenting on current events.

Following the duel, Burr, who now faced considerable hostility in New York City, went to Philadelphia. There reunited with a former lover, he wrote to his daughter, "If any male friend of yours should be dying of ennui, recommend him to engage in a duel and a courtship at the same time."

10

George Mason

No one of the Founding Fathers—not even Jefferson or Hamilton—was more paradoxical than George Mason. Few participants in the Constitutional Convention of 1787 spoke as often as he or exercised as much influence on the character of the great document. Yet when the time came for signing it, he said he "would sooner chop off his right hand than put it to the Constitution as it now stands."

There are other great paradoxes as well. One of the greatest is that few Americans—even educated ones—can identify him even though his image is seen every year by hundreds of thousands touring the Capitol of the United States. His marble portrait is one of those of the bringers of the law over the gallery doors of the House of Representatives, where it shares space with such world-famous figures as Hammurabi, Moses, Solon, Justinian, Maimonides, Alfonso X, Edward I, Grotius, and Blackstone. This was no isolated tribute to Mason's international stature. Jefferson, in his *Autobiography*, praised him as "a man of the first order of wisdom among those who acted on the theater of the Revolution, of expansive mind, profound judgment, cogent in argument, learned in the lore of our former constitution, and earnest for the republican change in democratic principles." Madison wrote that it was "to be regretted that, highly distinguished as he was, the memorials of [his accomplishments] on record or perhaps otherwise attainable are more scanty than of many of his contemporaries far inferior to him in intellectual prowess and in public service." Philip Mazzei, a sophisticated Italian who had a reading acquaintance with history's titans and personal friendships with many of Europe's and North America's great in his own time, praised Mason as "one of those brave, rare-talented men who cause Nature a great effort to produce—a Dante, a Machiavelli, a Galileo, a Newton, a Franklin."

As great a paradox as any is the fact that this Fairfax County squire, who labored for decades in the service of a community that widened from county to colony to nation to world, fought a life-long battle against lethargy; that this man who so dreaded speaking in public that he almost fainted when he did, should become one of the most frequent speakers in the Constitutional Convention of 1787 and at the conclusion of that illustrious conclave defy the majority that he had helped to build within its membership. Jefferson said that among debaters Mason was "most steadfast, able, and zealous." His career seems even more remarkable when one considers that throughout his busiest years he suffered not only from intensely painful gout and other very real diseases but seemingly from a host of imaginary ones. In another book, *Three Golden Ages*, I entitled the chapter on Mason "Heroic Hypochondriac."

There was trauma in his early life. In 1735, when he was ten years old, his father was drowned as a sudden storm sank a ferry plying the Potomac near their home. His mother, Ann Thomson Mason, was left with two children younger than George, a four-year-old girl and a two-year-old boy. She had sound judgment and managed successfully the large estate which she inherited. George's uncle, John Mercer, a prominent attorney, became coguardian of the children.

Despite the family's prosperity, the boy was not sent for advanced schooling to William and Mary or a college in any of the other colonies. But he was not disadvantaged in comparison with those youngsters who did, some of whom served with him later in Williamsburg and Philadelphia. Uncle John's library was one of the largest in Virginia and especially rich in legal lore. And the uncle himself was a bright and knowledgeable participant in public affairs. George Mason was a genius. Brilliant youngsters, even some lucky enough to obtain university training, sometimes discover in later years that a large family library and dinner table conversations constitute the most important parts of their education.

As he began to acquire a library of his own, he collected many of the world's most profound books and much of its greatest literature. Deep thinking became a habit, and the cadences of Shakespeare and Homer became part of his own style of expression.

In 1746, at the age of twenty-one, Mason succeeded to his estate and became at once one of the rich men of Virginia. Two years later he became a candidate for burgess from Fairfax County. He lost. No one assumed that this defeat would end his political career. His father and grandfather, each also named George Mason, had been vestrymen, churchwardens, gentlemen justices, and members of Virginia's House of Burgesses. As heir to that tradition, and rich besides, this George Mason stood an excellent chance of serving in the same positions. His political debut had been a bit premature, and he had skipped preliminary offices that might have prepared him for a role in Virginia's legislature.

The next spring, he offered as a candidate for the vestry of Truro Church, which served the Anglican parish of Fairfax County. As the functions of the vestry were matters of public administration

as well as religious service, the post would provide a good appren-
ticeship for training in political leadership beyond the local level.
Of the twelve men elected, Mason received the second highest vote.
A few months later, when a churchwarden died, Mason was chosen
to succeed him.

The port town of Dumfries was incorporated in Fairfax County
in the same year, and the twenty-four-year-old Mason was one of
seven men elected town trustees. Also in 1749, young Mason was
elected treasurer of the Ohio Company, a development company
granted a million acres of Virginia's western lands. Other directors
were from the Washington, Lee, Fairfax, Carter, Wormley, and
Tayloe families from the Old Dominion. These men played dominant roles in the colony. In 1751, they gained a new director destined to surpass the fame of all the others—a nineteen-year-old
George Washington.

By this time, Mason had been married about a year to Ann Eil-
beck, a Marylander described in the *Maryland Gazette*'s account of
their marriage as "a young lady of distinguishing merit and beauty,
and a handsome fortune." Twenty-three years later, Mason wrote in
the family Bible, "She was something taller than the middle size
and elegantly shaped. Her eyes were black, tender and lively, her
features regular and delicate; her complexion remarkably fair and
fresh—lilies and roses (almost without a metaphor) were blended
there—and a certain inexpressible air of cheerfulness, health, inno-
cence, and sensibility diffused over her countenance formed a face
the very reverse of what is generally called masculine." The bride
was sixteen. The groom was a stocky twenty-five-year-old whose
plump face was given force by bright brown eyes and black eyebrows.

When Mason wrote his description of Ann in the Bible, it was in
registration of her death, which he said occurred "in the thirty-
ninth year of her age, after a painful and tedious illness of more
than nine months, which she bore with truly Christian patience and
resignation, in faithful hope of eternal happiness in the world to
come." The inscription was such as any reverent planter or minister

of the gospel might have written. Mason's reputation for veracity and his habit of exact phraseology leave little doubt that his attitude was essentially Christian. We know that thirty-seven years as a vestryman and service as churchwarden do not necessarily signify adherence to Christianity in any conventional sense; these offices carry civil functions as well. His Bible entry is another matter. He was too much of an idealist to profane with an untruth the record of his beloved mate's death.

Equally suggestive of conventional piety is his habit, as reported by his son John, of saying grace, or having one of his sons say it, before each meal. The blessing was short and simple: "God bless us and what we are going to receive." John was a trustworthy witness. He wrote of his father affectionately but unsentimentally and without any effort to make him a plaster saint. In the same passage in which the son reported the custom of saying grace at table, he reported that his father at mealtime "was not morose but often taciturn. . . . I have frequently known his mind—though always kind and affectionate to his children—so diverted from the objects around him that he would not for days together miss one of the family that may have been absent, and would sometimes at table inquire for one of my sisters who had perhaps gone a week on a visit to some friends of which he had known but forgotten."

Twelve children had been born to George and Ann Mason. Nine survived to adulthood. Two years after his wife's death, Mason declined reelection to the House of Burgesses, citing "the duty I owe to a poor little helpless family of orphans to whom I must now act the part of Father and Mother both."

Even before he was a widower, the man who had once prematurely contended for a seat in the House of Burgesses had become notoriously reluctant to accept responsibilities that would keep him from home more than a day. He suffered from a complex variety of symptoms in addition to his increasingly painful gout.

The home that he was so reluctant to leave was one of the most beautiful in America. Mason and his brother had brought to the colony William Buckland, a young English architect who later became famous for the creation of handsome homes in Annapolis. The carving in the Palladian interior of Mason's Gunston Hall was unsurpassed anywhere in North America.

A disproportionate amount of the owner's time was spent in a single room, his study, across the hall from his bedroom. The architectural outlines and handsome furnishings of this chamber must often have been almost hidden by the debris of scholarly materials and public papers. John received requests from his father, away on public business, to send necessary papers from the study. George Mason did not recall on what piece of furniture they rested, but instructed him not to disturb the order of the layers, especially those in the window seats. In contrast to his confusion about the papers as physical entities, he had a distinct memory of their factual content.

From the age of thirty onward, Mason suffered from various illnesses that kept him not only at home but for long intervals in bed. He constantly studied contemporary problems in the light of history and sought to influence the course of events. But he preferred to exert influence as an advisor to such public men as his neighbor George Washington rather than as a prominent actor in events. Laziness played no part in Mason's withdrawal from activities that would keep him from home. He worked hard on numerous local projects for the community. When the contractor for construction of Pohick Church died in the midst of the project, Mason, as his executor, assumed the supervisory responsibilities of the dead man. Moreover, he personally directed all the activities of his vast estates without the customary help of administrative assistants.

When Parliament, responding to the demand of King George III, punished Boston for its famous Tea Party, the colonies were shocked by the severity of the Boston Port Bill, which prohibited the loading or unloading of ships in Boston Harbor. Mason was one of the leaders of a movement among Fairfax County citizens to provide money, flour, and wheat to relieve the suffering Bostonians. Mason composed the Fairfax Resolves, twenty-four resolutions that were read aloud by George Washington to an assembly of Fairfax citizens who enthusiastically adopted them. They became the model for resolutions adopted by other American communities. In them, Mason claimed for England's American colonists the rights of Englishmen enjoyed in England itself. He urged a boycott of English goods. One resolution demanded "an entire stop" to the "wicked, cruel, and unnatural" slave trade that had been encouraged by London. While affirming "in the strongest terms our duty and affection" to King and government, the protesters said that they were "most humbly conjuring and beseeching His Majesty not to reduce his faithful subjects of America to a state of desperation, and to reflect that from our Sovereign there can be but one appeal." Of course, that was the appeal to arms. Bold words from the recluse of Gunston Hall!

Mason's demand for an end to the slave trade was an expression of his religious conviction that slavery was, as he said in Biblical phraseology, "wicked." Though a slaveowner himself, Mason wanted to bring to an end the trade by which the institution flourished.

Mason's Fairfax Plan for boycott of British goods and the promotion of cooperation among the colonies became the model for the Virginia Association, the prototype of the Continental Association, which was the most important instrument forged by the Continental Congress.

After serving in the Virginia House of Burgesses, Mason had told his fellow citizens that the experience had been too disagreeable to repeat. Nevertheless, deeply concerned over the mounting crisis in relations between the colonies and the Crown, he yielded to the importunities of his neighbors and consented to serve in Virginia's third Revolutionary convention. The session convened in Richmond. Lord Dunmore, the royal governor, had fled Williamsburg. Patrick Henry had called for liberty or death. Blood had been shed in defense of liberty in Massachusetts. The Continental Congress had named Washington to command of the Revolutionary armies.

Historians look back to the 1775 Convention as an able assembly. But Mason, impatient with those less learned than he (that is, almost all of the human race) and less swift in the conduct of public business, was pricked by pain into frustration and irritability. He wrote Washington, "I never was in so disagreeable a situation, and almost despaired of a cause which I saw so ill-conducted. Mere vexation and disgust threw me into such an ill state of health that . . . I was sometimes near fainting in the House."

Mason nevertheless agreed to serve in the vital convention of 1776. He arrived late, however, because of an attack of the gout. By the time he appeared, his colleagues had already voted to instruct Virginia's delegates to the Continental Congress to introduce a resolution proposing a declaration of independence. North Carolina in this crucial year instructed its delegates to the Congress to support such a declaration if it were proposed, but Virginia was the only colony instructing its representatives to make the proposal. The Virginia convention entrusted the wording of the resolution for independence to a committee of thirty-four members. It also assigned them the task of preparing "a Declaration of Rights and such a plan of government as will be most likely to maintain peace and order in this colony, and secure substantial and equal liberty to the people."

Interestingly, many historians since that time have agreed that the Virginia Convention of 1776 was one of the ablest conclaves in American history.

On arrival, Mason was added to the already huge committee. No one in America, perhaps no one in the world, was better qualified for the task of writing a declaration of rights and a constitution. Among those aware of this fact was Mason himself. To Richard Henry Lee he wrote that the committee was "overcharged with useless members" and that consequently he, Mason, would have to deal with "a thousand ridiculous and impracticable proposals."

Edmund Pendleton reported to Thomas Jefferson that "The political cooks are busy in preparing the dish, and as Colonel Mason seems to have the ascendancy in the great work, I have sanguine hopes it will be framed so as to answer its end." Pendleton's hopes were fully justified. Within ten days the committee presented to the convention a declaration shaped by Mason's thoughts and bearing the stamp of his eloquence. The first paragraph declared "all men are created free and independent, and have certain inherent natural rights, of which they cannot, by any compact, deprive or divest their posterity." This statement provoked angry charges that it was an invitation to slaves to rebel. After several days of contention, the argument was settled by the addition of a single phrase so that the disputed portion asserted, "All men are by nature equally free and independent, and have certain inherent rights, of which, *when they enter into a state of society*, they cannot, by any compact deprive or divest their posterity."

After about two weeks of debate, on June 12, 1776, the convention unanimously adopted Mason's document, the Virginia Declaration of Rights. There were amendments that he reluctantly accepted, but the ratified document still carried its original thrust and expressed his political philosophy, mostly in his own memorable words. The change that caused him the most pain was the elimination of his words condemning slavery.

Mason was also disappointed by the amended version of his reference in Article 16 to "religion, or the duty which we owe to our divine and omnipotent Creator." Substituted for his original phrases were the words "religion, or the duty which we owe to our CREATOR." He evidently regarded the modified wording as a less robust statement of faith than his original.

Some subsequent commentators, while praising Mason's eloquence and erudition, have regretted that even in its final version the comments on religion are too exclusively oriented for a government document that should provide equal toleration for the atheist and the believer. Virtually no one has questioned its brilliance or denied its influence.

His regrets about the changed reference to the Deity were somewhat ameliorated by what he did successfully include in that paragraph: "Religion, or the duty which we owe to our CREATOR, and the manner of discharging it, can be directed only by reason and conviction, not by force or violence; and therefore all men are equally entitled to the free exercise of religion, according to the dictates of conscience; and . . . it is the mutual duty of all to practice Christian forbearance, love, and charity towards each other." Note that not just the initial letter of "CREATOR" is capitalized but every letter in the word. Note, too, that the practice of religion is referred to not merely as a right but as "the *duty* which we *owe* to our CREATOR." And the admonition is specifically to practice "*Christian* forbearance, love, and charity."

Anyone reading Mason's Declaration must feel very much like the teenager of our own time who expressed surprise that "a great writer like Shakespeare had used so many old familiar quotations." Though Mason's writing shows the influence of great thinkers among the ancient Greeks and Romans as well as later centuries, his words are familiar most of all because they have inspired so many other historical utterances. We have heard their echoes in the Declaration of Independence, the Constitution of the United States, Lincoln's Gettysburg Address, Franklin D. Roosevelt's Four Freedoms speech, and the Atlantic Charter subscribed to by President Roosevelt and Prime Minister Churchill.

An eminent twentieth-century legal scholar, Dean Roscoe Pound of the Harvard Law School, said, "The Virginia Bill of Rights of 1776 is the first and, indeed, is the model of a long line of politico-legal documents that have become the staple of American constitutional law. . . . Moreover, in actual application in the courts, the Bills of Rights, both in the Federal and in the State constitutions, are the most frequently invoked and constantly applied provisions of those instruments. Nor has the Virginia Bill of Rights been conspicuous only as a model. With all allowance for the historical documents that went before it, it must be pronounced a great creative achievement."

Historian George Bancroft considered Mason's contribution unique. "Other colonies," Bancroft wrote, "had framed bills of rights in reference to their relations with Britain; Virginia moved from charters and customs to primal principles, from the altercation about facts to the contemplation of immutable truth. She summoned the eternal laws of man's being to protest against all tyranny. The English petition of rights in 1688 was historic and retrospective; the Virginia declaration came out of the heart of nature, and announced governing principles for all peoples in all time. It was the voice of reason going forth to speak a new political world into being."

Edmund Randolph, then a member of the convention, later a member of Washington's cabinet, expressed in retrospect the essence of the historical moment when he said that the Declaration was issued so that "a perpetual standard should be erected, around which the people might really, and . . . be forever admonished to be watchful, firm, and virtuous" through "all the revolutions of time, human opinion, and government."

William C. Rives cited the Declaration as "a condensed, logical, and luminous summary of the great principles of freedom inherited by us . . . the extracted essence . . . distilled and concentrated through the alembic of [Mason's] own powerful and discriminating mind. There is nothing more remarkable in the political annals of America than this paper."

The effect, so long lasting, was also immediate. "By the time the last cannonade of the Revolution sounded," wrote Robert A. Rutland, "every state either had fashioned a separate bill of rights or had passed statutes with similar provisions. In a good many cases the work was done with scissors, pastepot, and a copy of the Virginia Declaration—a fact that did not escape Mason's notice."

The litany of praise for Mason's Virginia Declaration of Rights is long and the scroll is filled with shining names. But the best thing a reader can do upon finishing this chapter is to turn to the appendix of this volume and read the Declaration itself. Preliminary comments can aid in understanding the significance of the great document but are not an adequate substitute for direct experience of the document itself.

Hamilton James Eckenrode, in *Separation of Church and State in Virginia*, points out the dramatic effect of Mason's *Declaration* on government and religion in Virginia: "Prosecution for religious causes ceased. Disabilities on account of religion were removed. . . . Anglicans, Roman Catholics, Evangelicals, Jews, and unbelievers were placed on the same civil footing." Thus Virginia, he said, "was ahead of the world . . . making the first legal statement of the principle of religious liberty."

One of the most important effects of Mason's work was the inspiration with which it ignited other brilliant minds in his own time and later. As originally drafted and widely circulated, Mason's Declaration contained the word "toleration." Madison greatly admired the document, but was displeased that it called for "toleration." Daniel L. Dreisbach has neatly summarized the point at issue ("George Mason's Pursuit of Religious Liberty in Revolutionary Virginia," *Virginia Magazine of History and Biography*, vol. 108, pp. 5–44). He says, "In Madison's mind, the right of religious exercise was too important to be cast in the form of a mere privilege allowed by the ruling polity and enjoyed as a grant of governmental benevolence. Instead, he viewed religious liberty as a fundamental and irrevocable right, possessed equally by all citizens, that must be placed beyond the reach of civil magistrates."

Mason's words had not only fueled the thoughts of other intellectuals but also had fired the imaginations and aspirations of ordinary citizens. The Presbyterians of Prince Edward County hailed the last article of the Bill of Rights as "the rising sun of religious liberty, to relieve us from a long night of ecclesiastical bondage, and we do most earnestly request and expect that you would go on to complete what is so nobly begun, raise religious as well as civil liberty to the zenith of glory, and make Virginia an asylum for free enquiry, knowledge, and the virtuous of every denomination." They urged the legislature to "pull down all church establishments." The legislators received similar appeals from Baptists and other groups of worshipers. As we have seen in earlier chapters, this feat, with the aid of Madison and Jefferson, was decisively accomplished. As a Virginia legislator, Mason was a vital part of all the legislation defining relations between church and state.

The Constitution of Virginia prepared by Mason became a model for those adopted in other states and even for the federal constitution. At the constitutional convention in Philadelphia he was, despite his pain, the threat of fainting, and the excruciating insecurity that afflicted him, one of the three most frequent speakers—and one of the most effective. Ironically, though he played so important a role in making the Constitution of the United States and was author of the world's most influential bill of rights, he was unable to insert a bill of rights in the new instrument of government. Commenting on Mason's actions after so dramatically refusing to sign, Madison said that his fellow delegate "left Philadelphia in an exceeding ill humor indeed."

Mason did not give up the fight. With Patrick Henry and William Grayson, he fought against ratification in Virginia's ratifying convention and almost succeeded. Fortunately, in light of subsequent events, the Constitution survived—and under the best circumstances. In order to defeat the efforts of the anti-ratification forces, the Constitution's supporters pledged that they would work to amend the document to include a bill of rights.

They kept their promise. On September 25, 1789, the first Congress of the United States, in the first session, acted to submit to the individual states a series of amendments designed to protect individual and state rights. A sufficient number of states ratified ten of the proposed amendments to add them to the Constitution. They constituted the Bill of Rights. The first of these amendments provided that "Congress shall make no law respecting an establishment of religion, or prohibiting the free exercise thereof; or abridging the freedom of speech, or of the press; or the right of the people peaceably to assemble, and to petition the Government for a redress of grievances." The words lacked the eloquence and inspirational force of Mason's Declaration, but in dispassionate lawyerly language they set forth the same principles which he had advocated.

Mason's services to democratic government, and especially to religious freedom, were not confined to his early activities in the Virginia legislature and in the Constitutional Convention of 1787.

At various times in the years between 1776 and 1788, he was a watchdog for liberty, especially religious liberty. Perhaps his second marriage, in 1780, to Sarah Brent, member of a prominent Catholic family, intensified his sensitivity to the rights of religious minorities.

He was a powerful warrior for liberty but by no means a prototype of William Wordsworth's "Happy Warrior," eager for a good fight for a great cause. Mason fought a great fight for a great cause, and he triumphed magnificently. But every step of the way he fought battles with himself, ignoring his pains, conquering his fears, and whipping himself on to a necessary labor at odds with his retiring nature and tortured psyche.

Religion obviously was one of the most important elements in George Mason's life. The question of religious freedom was sometimes the only thing that brought him out of retirement from public life, the only thing that brought him back to the arena despite pains, illness, and flagging spirits. It made him a formidable debater in spite of the physical faintness against which he struggled when speaking in public. What would George Mason have been without his faith? There is almost nothing to support the supposition that, without religion, he would have been a public menace, employing his genius in wicked ways to gain selfish ends. Doubtless, with or without faith, he would have been restrained by moral considerations. But, without religion, he might have been a useless recluse nursing his pain and his wrath, or a sarcastic misanthrope. Instead, he is one of the greatest benefactors in world history.

11

Charles Carroll of Carrollton

ONE of the most religious of America's Founding Fathers was the son of an intensely religious man who deliberately fathered him illegitimately. The parental motivation counted any stigma of bastardy as an inconvenience to be ignored for the sake of religion and family tradition. When the son became the richest man in colonial Maryland, and one of the most powerful, he was still denied the right to hold office or even to vote. This man was Charles Carroll of Carrollton, the last living signer of the Declaration of Independence and the only Catholic among the fifty-eight signers.

The signer was the third Charles in his direct line of American descent. The experiences of Charles the immigrant and of his Irish forebears shaped the determination of his son, Charles of Annapolis, to have an illegitimate son. The siring of an illegal heir was a long-contemplated, carefully planned project. The rearing of the son, who called himself Charles Carroll of Carrollton to distinguish himself from relatives of the same name, was also designed to produce an unusual offspring.

The boy destined to be a Founding Father was born on September 19, 1737, in Annapolis, Maryland. After more than a century and a half of gossip followed by many decades of evasive or inaccurate historical accounts, the essential facts surrounding the birth were revealed in publications by Ronald Hoffman, notably in the year 2000, in his *Princes of Ireland, Planters of Maryland, A Carroll Saga*.

Charles the immigrant, often called Charles the Settler, sailed to Maryland with the idea of rebuilding the status of his family, once the breeder of ruling princes in Ireland, now part of a persecuted minority reduced to servility in their own homeland. He implanted the same dedication in his son, Charles of Annapolis. With this second Charles it became an obsession, one raised almost to manic levels by the frustration of enduring second-class citizenship when he was the richest man in Maryland.

He determined to rear a son fitted by character, ability, and education to contend successfully with the Protestant majority in Maryland for a position of leadership unsurpassed by anyone else. With the family's wealth, energy, and intelligence, they could have moved quickly to the front rank of leadership by the simple expedient of converting to Anglicanism. Many Catholics in Maryland had, including its founders, the Calverts. But both Charles the Settler and Charles of Annapolis were adamant that their religious allegiance was not for sale. They were equally determined that the Carrolls should once again occupy the position of power and prestige that they had enjoyed for generations before the Protestant triumph.

So a mixture of family pride, personal ambition, and religious fealty impelled Charles Carroll of Annapolis to resort to an unusual experiment. He would breed a son from good stock, imbue him with a proper sense of loyalty to family and church, and give him the best educational opportunities that Western civilization could provide. But if a wife proved incapable of providing a male heir or if the young man proved inadequate to his assigned task, the entire scheme would be thwarted. Charles Carroll of Annapolis did not want to be married to someone incapable of providing the heir that he sought, nor did he wish to settle his estate upon an heir unable to fill his intended role. Neither mother nor son should automatically be his heir. If his first experiment failed, he would try again under other circumstances. He decided to proceed without the binding restriction of marriage.

So he entered into an intimate relationship with Elizabeth Brooke, his cousin, who had been reared as Catholic and had three great-uncles who were Jesuit priests. Not until November 1756, when the resulting child, Charles Carroll of Carrollton, was nineteen, did his mother and father legalize their union. By then, young Charles had spent sixteen years in Europe, separated from his family, in order to obtain an education that, joined with his wealth, would make him advantaged above other Marylanders of his generation.

The elder Charles Carroll sent his son to Europe at the age of ten. The boy was enrolled in the English Jesuit school at St. Omer in French Flanders. For sixteen years, he would live in Europe, apart from his family, attending one school after another. The letters he exchanged with his parents reveal great loneliness on the part of the child and affection on the part of the parents, especially the mother. The child's longing for his family, relieved by a single visit from the father, was expressed poignantly in a comment following his mother's death when he was twenty-four. He wrote, "Those happy days spent . . . in her sweet company, our lonely retirement and mutual fondness, pass in remembrance before me. I shall never see such days again."

When twenty-two-year-old Charley, as the son was familiarly

known, was in school in London, his father cautioned him to avoid "the women of the town" as he "would a rattlesnake." He warned, "I have known some young men, after as much time and money spent on their education as has been on yours, snatched from their expecting parents by the poison received from prostitution. Others I have known long to linger in a state of rottenness and at last to die objects of horror. Therefore, if the more noble and pure sentiments of virtue and duty should fail to keep you innocent, let a regard to your health deter you from a crime, which may in this world make you most miserable."

The father must not have been completely reassured by Charley's promise that he would not "think of marriage without" his sire's "previous consent and knowledge." The young man also volunteered that he found nothing as "engaging as women" and "wondered why Providence had bestowed such art, such sagacity, on that sex and at the same time so much beauty."

Charley's father conceded that his son had attained an age at which "it is natural to think of" union with a member of the opposite sex. But the older man described it as a process of "establishing yourself in the world by marriage." He told Charley to seek someone not only "virtuous, sensible, good natured, complaisant, complying, and of a cheerful disposition" but from a family of prestige comparable to his own. Her fortune must be comparable to his. He warned that Charley must not "marry a Protestant, for beside the risk your offspring will run, it is certain there cannot be any solid happiness without a union of sentiments in all matters, especially in religion."

The senior Charles softened his admonitions with the concession that he would not object if Charley "should condescend to take a woman unequal to you in point of fortune" if the "inequality [was] compensated in point of family [and] by her virtue and the other qualities of her mind and person."

Throughout Charley's stay abroad, his father's letters were an intermittent flow of professed love combined with stern demands for continued advancement and reminders of future rewards. The father's letter of October 10, 1753, to the sixteen-year-old school-boy was typical. The elder Carroll acknowledged receipt of the boy's letters over the preceding fourteen months. He assured his son that they were "all most welcome to me, and although a hurry of business prevents my often writing to you, you may be assured you are always in my thoughts and that I most earnestly wish your happiness. As you have no such avocations, I desire I may often hear from you. . . . With your mother, I shall be glad to have your picture in the compass of 15 inches by 12."

So much for parental pleasantries. "Dear child, I long to see you, but I did not send you so far only to learn a little Greek and Latin. Where you are, you can only lay a foundation for other studies which may hereafter be profitable to yourself and useful to your friends. When you have gone through them, the rest of your life will be a continued scene of ease and satisfaction, if you keep invariably in the paths of truth and virtue. The husbandman annually repeats the toil of dressing, plowing and sowing for his harvest. When you have completed higher studies, your toil will be over, and your harvest will always and daily come in."

He added, "Mr. Wappeler informs me you are third in your school, which gives me great pleasure, and as your judgment unfolds itself and ripens, I expect to hear of your still rising. . . . If you do, it will afford me the greatest comfort and satisfaction and increase the love I have for you."

When Charley graduated from St. Omer's at age sixteen, the master wrote the boy's father that he had "lost this morning the finest young man, in every respect, that ever entered the house. . . . I find the public voice confirms my private sentiment."

Charley's father now felt sure that he had bred a son fit to maintain the family honor and influence in a colony dominated by Protestants. But he was not yet ready to have his son return home. More education abroad was necessary to fit him for high responsibilities in a precarious location. Charley was disappointed, but the master marveled that he revealed no resentment. He neglected neither his books nor his devotions.

When he had completed courses of instruction at the College of the English Jesuits at St. Omer in French Flanders and studied poetry for a year in the College of French Jesuits at Rheims, followed by two years of universal philosophy at the College of Louis-le-Grand in Paris, he entered upon five years of legal studies at the Inner Temple in London. Papa had wanted his son to acquire broad learning but had regarded the law as the most important of his pursuits. He relied on the combination of wealth and legal expertise to preserve and expand the family influence. But his son hated legal studies and failed to distinguish himself as he had in other disciplines. When he was twenty-five years old, his father permitted him to return home.

Charley's father was dissatisfied with his life in Maryland. Though he was the richest man in the colony, his status as a loyal Catholic deprived him of privileges enjoyed by the mass of citizens. From time to time, he considered selling much of his Maryland property and moving to Louisiana, which had a large Catholic population.

Charley, on the other hand, was delighted to be going home, first of all to see his family but also to return to his native colony. True, he had not seen it since he was a child, but he had happy memories of it and it may have been made dearer by his sixteen years of exile. He lamented that his mother, whom he had longed to see, had died during what he called his "banishment." His father was lavish in praise of "a most tender mother" and "the best of wives."

At age twenty-eight, however, Charles had little time for dwelling in the past. His father turned over to his management ten thousand acres of the family estate. His father expected him to do more than maintain or, better still, increase the profitability of the land. He was also to use the knowledge and skills obtained in a formal education such as few Americans had known and, with these advantages, to gain for himself and his coreligionists political influence on a scale such as they had not known since the Calverts had ruled Maryland while remaining true to the old faith.

Some might suppose that, having been trained principally by Jesuit priests in Catholic schools, all the while feeling the threat of persecution, young Carroll would be ill-equipped to understand important aspects of a Protestant society. Such was not the case. His father had made sure that his son, even as a teenager, was exposed to non-Catholic thought. In his letters, the elder Carroll had recommended to him not only the works of Catholic theologians but also of such controversial thinkers as Locke, Newton, and Montesquieu. He even suggested, for his son's reading, such works from the Pope's *Index Expurgatorius* as the writings of Voltaire. Before Charley's twenty-fifth birthday, Papa had warned him that he must not only eschew any action "contrary to morality, justice, and religion" but also any rules or doctrines "inconsistent with reason." As Charles entered upon his new responsibilities, he was sustained by his traditional faith and energized by the prospect of serving his colony so well with his wealth and his talents as to overcome the opposition of bigotry.

He proved an effective manager of his large properties but, like his father, he was barred from political activity because of his Catholicism. Like such other Americans of his time as Jefferson, Madison, Adams, and Mason, he acquired a large library including many works on history and political philosophy. But unlike these compatriots, Carroll seemed to have little prospect of applying the lessons he learned. A Catholic who refused to abandon his faith or even disguise it had less political power than any white Protestant male who met the minimum property requirement. Such a man, stumbling up half-inebriated, his brow corrugated in concentration, his shifting tongue working as hard as the hand with which he made his mark on a citizen's petition, was exercising a privilege denied to the exquisitely educated Charles Carroll of Carrollton.

Like Madison, he was short, slender, and frail-looking. When he was about to marry Mary Darnall, a first cousin once removed who was twelve years his junior, he wrote to a friend that she was "a little too young for me . . . especially as I am of a weak and puny constitution." He described his fiancée as a "sweet tempered, charming, neat girl," "virtuous and sensible." As for looks, he assured one correspondent that his intended's "person" was "agreeable and cleanly." Not surprisingly, in view of his "exile" between the ages of ten and twenty-six, he seems to have been reticent about love.

Meanwhile he fulfilled the responsibilities of a husband, a wealthy planter and businessman, and a socially prestigious host. But he was not allowed to fulfill the responsibilities of a citizen.

Events in 1770 gave him a chance to earn the opportunity. The two houses of the Maryland Assembly were locked in combat over proposed legislation regulating the fees for officers of the Crown and the stipends for the clergy of the Established Church. The lower house wished to reform the whole fee system. The upper house vehemently resisted. Royal Governor Eden prorogued the legislature and proclaimed continuation of the status quo. Wealthy men tended to support his position, but Carroll was opposed. He resented being taxed to support a church of which he was not a member—indeed, a church whose adherents denied him the privilege of voting.

The issues of 1770 were still bitterly contested in 1773. A letter supporting the royal governor's position was published in the *Maryland Gazette* over the pseudonym Antilon. The public, apparently correctly, assumed that the letter writer was Daniel Dulany. Like Carroll, Dulany was the grandson of an Irish immigrant, but he was a Protestant, a member of the governor's council, and the deputy secretary of Maryland's royal government. In this Crown office, he earned fees that many people considered exorbitant. A skilled attorney, he presented his views in the form of a dialogue between two citizens. First Citizen was an opponent of the royal governor's stance. Second Citizen was a defender of royal prerogatives. First Citizen was made to blunder in his presentation. Second Citizen, Dulany's mouthpiece, easily demolished the arguments of the First Citizen.

Soon a letter signed First Citizen appeared in the *Maryland Gazette*. First Citizen had emerged from the role of blunderer and adroitly carved up the arguments of Second Citizen, who now appeared rather stupid. Perceptive readers correctly suspected that another intellect now animated First Citizen. Some realized that Carroll, a skilled debater, had cleverly assumed the identity that Dulany had assigned to a shallow character of his own invention.

For five months, the argument was waged in the newspaper, with both parties displaying considerable erudition. Dulany continued to use the pen name Antilon, enduring the frustration of assaults by a character of his own invention who now served as Carroll's puppet. On one level the verbal fireworks were an exhibition of sparkling wit and coruscating elements of Western culture. On another, they descended to personal invective that seldom soared to subtlety beyond the arc of a lobbed firecracker.

Carroll's father, delighted with the prowess of the son he had shaped for leadership, wrote to him: "A gentleman told me you appeared at the county court on Friday, that the whisper immediately ran, 'There is the first citizen,' and that every eye was fixed on you with evident marks of pleasure and approbation, that many said they did not know which to admire most, your strength of reasoning or your calm and gentleman-like style."

Charley Carroll was not always as calm as his father thought. He smarted under the insinuations of Dulany's epistolary allies, who publicly sympathized with their friend for being subjected to the "holy inquisition of Jesuits" through the insults of a "nursling of St. Omer." One attacked "First Citizen" as a man determined to "make way for popery . . . a complication of all the absurdities, rogueries, and errors that ever appeared among men, or that the craft, folly, and malice of men is capable of." Dulany's brother insulted both Carrolls, father and son, in such terms that Charley issued a challenge and rode out to duel with him, only to find that his opponent had failed to appear after referring to the challenger as a "silly little puppy."

Still Carroll had gained considerable prestige from the war of words in the press. Many Marylanders—Protestant as well as Catholic—considered the actions of royal officials inexcusably high-handed. Though Carroll did not yet have a vote, he was influencing those who did. In the legislative campaign of May 1773, his letters as First Citizen were cited again and again. His endorsement was sought by candidates impatient with royal paternalism. It was generally conceded that at least one candidate owed his victory principally to his alliance with Carroll.

When the newly elected Maryland House was split into three factions—status quo, moderate reform, and radical reform—the moderates sought a compromise with the royal governor on reformation of the fee system. They wanted Carroll's advice and the support of his pen. This group included Samuel Chase, William Paca, Thomas Johnson, and Matthew Tilghman, men headed for dominant roles in Maryland politics. Aware of Carroll's rapidly growing influence, some enemies hurled anti-Catholic epithets at him, but this time the public paid little attention. Concentrating on enemies in Annapolis and London, they had no time for the revival of old quarrels with Rome.

When non-importation societies were formed to boycott products from the mother country as a protest against imperial exploitation, Carroll was prominent in leadership. With his wealth and expensive lifestyle, he had been a large importer. There were no religious barriers to his holding office in an organization opposing rather than implementing royal measures. When Annapolis patriots named a Committee of Correspondence to communicate with similar committees in other colonies, so that a united front might be built against what they regarded as tyranny, Carroll became one of the foremost leaders. He soon became prominent in the larger Committee of Correspondence serving all of Maryland. When the royal governor was forced to evacuate Maryland and a Committee of Safety was appointed to succeed him and his council, Carroll was a valuable member.

His service soon became continental. In February 1776, when the Continental Congress appointed a three-member commission to visit Canada "to promote or form a union" between it and the American colonies to the south, Carroll—though not a congressman—was one of the emissaries. The others were Samuel Chase and Benjamin Franklin. Ordinarily all members of the commission would have been congressmen, but there were special reasons for naming Carroll. Because of his long residence in France and education in French schools, he had a knowledge of the French language equaled by few of his compatriots. French, of course, was the primary language of many Canadians. Moreover, Carroll's Catholic faith and background might inspire confidence among the many Canadian Catholics. The faith that had been an impediment to political advancement had now become an asset.

The mission, through no fault of the three commissioners, was a failure. Situations within Canada doomed the effort. But Carroll became well known to Franklin and drew the attention of other congressmen.

As a member of the Maryland Convention of 1776, Carroll was strongly influential in passage of a resolution calling for formal separation from Great Britain. A grateful people elected him to the Continental Congress. He worked successfully to have the Maryland Assembly rescind its instructions to delegates to oppose independence. In Philadelphia, on August 2, he signed the Declaration of Independence.

Today many people assume that all who signed the Declaration affixed their signatures on July 4. The signing was actually a drawn-out process, with many signing at their convenience rather than queueing up in a dramatic ceremony. There is no truth in the story that, at his signing, he added the words "of Carrollton" to his signature so that none of his relatives with the same name would be held responsible. He had added "of Carrollton" upon first assuming control of the estate which his father gave him. It is true that, in signing the Declaration, he endangered both his property and his life.

While a member of Congress, he served on the Board of War, which oversaw the Revolutionary armies and the supplying of their needs. He was dedicated to the causes of American independence, but he knew that excesses could be committed in the name of the religion called democracy as readily as in the name of any faith tolerated by ecclesiastical tradition. He wrote his father that, unless men of honor could bring stability to the government of Maryland, "anarchy will follow as a certain consequence, injustice, rapine, and corruption in the seats of justice will prevail, and this Province in a short time will be involved in all the horrors of an ungovernable and revengeful Democracy and will be dyed with the blood of its best citizens." In this warning, he was more insightful than some other patriots. This was partly because of his keen intelligence and his superior acquaintance with the world of banks and first-hand experience in other nations. He may also have been especially aware of the threat of instability because he was a very rich man. He had a lot to lose.

His own financial status may also have influenced his sympathetic attitude toward Englishmen threatened with confiscation of their American property. But he does seem to have been of that minority of the persecuted whose personal sufferings foster within them a sympathy for others who are oppressed rather than a desire to persecute in their turn. He pointed out that confiscation of Englishmen's property would make Americans guilty of the same actions which they had despised.

Carroll was influential in the making of Maryland's constitution. As always, he was attentive to freedom of religion and freedom of expression.

Meanwhile, his prestige grew within the Congress. One day John Adams recorded in his diary his meeting with "a Mr. Carrell (sic) of Annapolis, a very sensible gentleman, a Roman Catholic, and of the first fortune in America." Carroll's congressional colleagues continued to be impressed with his tremendous wealth and the fact that he was the only Catholic in their membership. But increasingly they were also impressed with the fact that he was indeed "a very sensible gentleman" and one whose vision had been broadened by his lengthy education in Europe. Furthermore, his earlier position as simultaneously a financial titan and a member of a victimized minority had given him a vision of the threats and promises of liberty that was unique among the most prominent Founding Fathers. He understood both the promises and the persecutions of a republican society, and he was ever mindful of the need for safeguards as well as opportunities. As the most influential Catholic in America and at the same time one of its most respected patriots, he helped to bridge the gap between Catholic and Protestant that George Washington strove to close.

Though Carroll was active in molding and securing the constitution of Maryland, being particularly protective of religious freedom, he declined to serve in the Convention of 1787 that produced the Constitution of the United States. Nevertheless, he worked for ratification of the new instrument of government, swaying many doubters in Maryland and influencing many fellow Catholics in other states to a degree that no one else matched.

He served as a U.S. senator under the new government, earning the public trust as an intelligent man, learned in the philosophy of government, and wise in the ways of business—above all one who could be trusted to put honor above personal advantage. His ethics were rooted in the faith in which he had been reared. Most of his instruction in its tenets had been the work of the Jesuit priests who were his teachers. This was what his father wanted. When his son was twenty-five years old, the elder Carroll wrote him, "I have, I thank God, been bred among them, and if you do what they have taught you and nothing contrary to it, you will be happy here and hereafter."

He wanted his son to be enthusiastic about Jesuit ways but not to the point of becoming a priest and thus defeating the paternal plan to produce a son who would restore past glories of a princely line. Ronald Hoffman, the able editor of the Carroll family papers, makes the point that the elder Carroll not only saw instruction in the faith as valuable in itself but also "viewed religious observance as a critical tool for enjoining discipline and imposing order on one's life." He cautioned his son that all too easily "business company" and "late hours" can gradually seem excuses for "first postponing and then neglecting our prayers, and this rampart being once overthrown, it's impossible to enumerate the sad toxin of evils which inevitably enter at the breach."

There is no evidence that the son's religious beliefs differed radically from the father's. The elder Carroll had not had as extensive a formal education as the son, but he had read a fair amount of Enlightenment literature. He was not parochial.

In 1800, at the age of sixty-three, Charles Carroll of Carrollton retired from public offices to devote himself to the management of his vast estates, which totaled between seventy thousand and eighty thousand acres in Maryland, Pennsylvania, and New York. But his interest in public enterprises continued. Having helped to lay the political foundations of his country, he now played a significant role in building its economic structure. In an era of western growth and demands for more efficient transportation, he was a prominent member of the Chesapeake & Ohio Canal Company. He was on the organizing board of the Baltimore and Ohio Railroad and took great satisfaction in personally laying the cornerstone on July 4, 1828. He was the last survivor among the signers of the Declaration of Independence, Jefferson and Adams having died two years before to the day. The man who had begun public life as a victim of religious discrimination in his native Maryland was now, at the age of ninety-one, a symbol of national unity.

His career had been largely one of conservative integrity, if it is not an oxymoron to speak of a conservative revolutionary. In at least one important respect, however, he was a liberal far ahead of many of his contemporaries, North as well as South. As early as 1797 he had introduced in the Maryland Senate a proposal for the gradual abolition of slavery. But there was insufficient support to accomplish his purpose. In 1832, William Lloyd Garrison, the Massachusetts abolitionist, made a harsh attack on Carroll as the owner of many inherited slaves and their multiplying progeny. "And yet," he complained, "he is lauded beyond measure as a patriot, a philanthropist, and a Christian." As biographer Joseph Gurn later pointed out, Carroll had worked for emancipation before the birth of his twenty-seven-year-old accuser.

What faith sustained Charles Carroll through the loneliness of his youth, the triumph of young manhood, and the challenges that persisted till his death on November 14, 1832, at the age of ninety-five? On his deathbed he received holy communion. His eyes were closed, but his hands moved gracefully in an act so habitual as not to require the guidance of sight. Immediately after, when his physician urged him to eat to gain a little strength, the patriot said, "Thank you, Doctor, not just now; this ceremony is so deeply interesting to the Christians that it supplies all the wants of nature. I feel no desire for food." He died that night without a struggle. The story may seem almost too pat to be true, but it is amply attested, even by one who did not share his faith.

This well-verified anecdote tells much about the old patriot's faith, but in every society there is a long history of deathbed conversions. Fortunately, there is much evidence to support the conclusion that religious faith had long been a powerful influence in his life, affecting both his private and public activities. One of the most impressive pieces of evidence is his refusal to abandon public loyalty to his denomination in order to gain the privilege of ordinary citizenship.

We have at least two pertinent declarations of faith in his own handwriting. The first was written on October 24, 1800, the year Jefferson was elected president of the United States. Twenty-four years earlier, Carroll had been proud to sign the Declaration of Independence authored by the Virginian. Subsequently, some of the Marylander's conservative friends feared that he was being influenced too much by the liberal Jefferson. Now he himself was fearful that Jefferson and his followers would make dangerously radical changes in American government—alterations based on the institutions of France.

Carroll's highly vocal support of Federalism had brought harsh criticism from many parts of his state. One night while traveling during this difficult period, he was forced by a thunderstorm to take shelter in "a poor cottage" where supper consisted entirely of "boiled Irish potatoes and milk." He wrote to his son, also named Charles, "It occurred to me that in the course of a few years I might be driven into exile by the prevalence of an execrable faction, and forced to shelter in as poor a hovel the remnant of a life, a considerable part of which had been faithfully devoted to my country's service." If this sounds a little paranoid, we must remember that Charles Carroll of Carrollton's father had reared him to be acutely conscious of the persecution that generations of his family had suffered and to be the dedicated instrument of triumph over the forces of oppression that had handicapped them and their fellow Catholics.

Carroll's great material successes had brought no dependable sense of security. He was warning his son not to put his trust in treasures laid up upon earth. Instead of citing the warnings of the Sermon on the Mount, however, he turned to a pre-Christian classic, Homer's *Odyssey*, referring to

the wise lesson of Ulysses to one of the suitors. It is well worth your perusal and observance; the poetry is fine, the advice worthy the wisdom of the much enduring and experienced man, and the morality truly sublime. Such reflections are necessary and should be frequently entertained in times like these, by men whose present prospects are promising. They serve to prepare the mind for adversities, and enable us to bear frowns and snubs of fortune with resignation and fortitude. A mind thus lectured and tutored will derive self-satisfaction from the consciousness that it will remain firm and unbroken in the midst of adverse storms. Can the pitiful pleasure resulting from a fine equipage and the gratifications of wealth, which the greatest villains may enjoy, be compared with this firm and steady temper of the mind, and its advantages?

The Jesuits had tutored Charles Carroll well in the Greek and Latin classics. Given Jesuit interpretations of the principal Greek and Roman thinkers, there was no conflict between their teachings and those of the Christian Bible. The priests saw the most enlightened of the ancients as precursors of Christianity, inhabiting a deeply shadowed alcove of history but perceiving from the edges of the not-yet-opened door some gleams of inspiration from the glory to come.

The next letter about his faith that we have, also written to his son, was dated November 4, 1800, just eleven days after the first one. He said, "Divine revelation has been scoffed at by the philosophers of the present day, the immortality of the soul treated as the dreams of fools or the invention of knaves, and death has been declared by public authority an eternal sleep; these opinions are gaining ground among us and silently sapping the foundations of a religion [that is] the encouragement of the good, the terror of evildoers, and the consolation of the poor, the miserable, and the distressed. Remove the hope and dread of future rewards and punishments, the most powerful restraint on wicked actions, and the strongest inducement to virtuous ones is done away."

Acknowledging the force of a common argument, he wrote,

Virtue may be said to be its own reward; I believe it to be so and even in this life the only source of happiness; and this intimate and necessary connection between virtue and happiness here and between vice and misery, is to my mind one of the surest pledges of happiness or misery in a future state of existence. But how few practice virtue for its own reward. Some of happy disposition and temperament, calm, reflecting men, exempt in a great degree from the turbulence of passions, may be virtuous for virtue's sake; small, however, is the number who are guided by reason alone, and who can always subject their passions to its dictates! He who can thus act may be said to be virtuous; but reason is often enlisted on the side of the passions, or at best, when most wanted, is weakest.

Hence, he said,

the necessity of a superior motive for acting virtuously; now,

what motive can be stronger than the belief, founded on revelation, that a virtuous life will be rewarded by a happy immortality? Without morals a republic cannot subsist any
length of time; they therefore, who are decrying the Christian religion, whose morality is so sublime and pure, which
denounces against the wicked, the eternal misery, and insures
to the good eternal happiness, are undermining the solid
foundations of morals, the best security for the duration of
free governments.

Near the end of what he himself called "a long, preaching letter," Carroll said, "My only hope is in that Being who educes good
out of evil; may He in His abundant mercy incline the hearts of our
countrymen to peace, justice and concord."

The third letter that we may cite as revelatory of Carroll's religious views shows him equally strong in religious convictions. In
this one, however, his views have a stronger denominational cast. It
was written on August 29, 1816, to his daughter-in-law Hattie. Carroll liked and respected her, but he had tried to prevent her from
marrying his son. Eventually he had capitulated in good grace to
the desires of the two young people. His letters to Hattie are affectionately phrased. His only objection to her had been the fact that
she was a Protestant. He feared for the future of his grandchildren:
With obvious relief, Carroll wrote,

> I am much gratified by your assurances that your daughters
> shall be brought up in the Roman Catholic religion; it is my
> wish and their father's also that they should be . . . though at
> present he has little religion himself, he is quite in earnest
> that his daughters should be religious; he as many others
> under the influence of passions know and feel the impor-
> tance of religion though they do not live up to its precepts.

Many readers in the twenty-first century will find a note of
smugness in Carroll's assumption that conscientious people who

failed to agree with him in religious matters differed because of a defect in their education. This idea is a far cry from Judge Learned Hand's assertion that "The spirit of liberty is the spirit which is not too sure that it is right." Perhaps Carroll's fight for survival in a society dominated by those intolerant of his faith did not admit of equivocation.

In any event, he did remain true to his own concept of religious toleration. He seems to have been true to his own declaration that he felt "no ill will or illiberal prejudices" against those who "abandoned" his faith "if their lives be conformable to the duties and morals prescribed by the Gospel." Also there was at least as much charity as narrowness in his hope and belief that such people would "be rewarded with eternal happiness."

All in all, Carroll was not one of those who abandoned Christian charity in pursuit of Christian conformity. He embraced, with no apparent sense of disturbing dichotomy, both the discoveries of the Enlightenment and the admonitions of traditional faith.

Though apparently consistently loyal to his Catholic faith, he was not always uncritical of its servants: To his best friend, William Graves, he wrote (August 15, 1774), "I execrate the intolerating spirit of the Church of Rome." Of the Jesuits, who had provided most of his formal instruction, he wrote to his father (October 22, 1761), "No one has a greater regard for the Jesuits than myself. I revere the virtue, I esteem the learning, I respect the apostolic labors of individuals but am forced to acknowledge their institute and plan of government liable to great abuses." He deplored "the extensive, too extensive, privileges conferred by former Popes on that order." He believed "dangerous to the state a body of men who . . . believe the dictates of one Superior, and are carried on to the execution of his orders with a blind impetuosity of will and eagerness to obey without the least enquiry or examination." Perhaps he would not have written so frankly to anyone other than a Catholic of proven loyalty, perhaps not even to anyone other than his beloved father.

He wrote, October 30, 1769, to his son,

I deem it my duty to call your attention to the shortness of this life, and the certainty of death, and the dreadful judgment we must all undergo, and on the decision of which a happy or a miserable eternity depends. The impious has said in his heart, 'There is no God.' He would willingly believe there is no God; the passions, the corruptions of the heart would fain persuade him there is none. The stings of conscience betray the emptiness of the delusion; the heavens proclaim the existence of God, and unperverted reason teaches that He must love virtue and hate vice, and reward the one and punish the other.

He concluded,

The wisest and best of the ancients believed in the immortality of the soul, and the Gospel has established the great truth of a future state of rewards and punishments. My desire to induce you to reflect on futurity, and by a virtuous life to merit heaven, have suggested the above reflections and warnings. The approaching festival of Easter, and the merits and mercies of our Redeemer . . . have led me into this chain of meditation and reasoning, and have inspired me with the hope of finding mercy before my Judge, and of being happy in the life to come, a happiness I wish you to participate [in] with me by infusing into your heart a similar hope. Should this letter produce such a change, it will comfort me, and impart to you that peace of mind which the world cannot give, and which I am sure you have long since ceased to enjoy.

He signed, "God bless you, from your affectionate father, Charles Carroll of Carrollton."

In September 1825, he wrote significantly in another vein about his religion. To his friend Charles W. Wharton he said:

> On the 20th of this month I entered into my eighty-ninth year. . . . This in any country would be deemed a long life, yet . . . if it has not been directed to the only end for which man was created, it is a mere nothing, an empty phantom, an indivisible point, compared with eternity.
>
> Too much of my time and attention have been misapplied on matters to which an impartial Judge, penetrating the secrets of hearts, before whom I shall soon appear, will ascribe [no] merit deserving recompense. On the mercy of my redeemer I rely for salvation, and on his merits; not on the works I have done in obedience to his precepts, for even these, I fear, a mixture of alloy will render unavailing and cause to be rejected.

Throughout most of Carroll's long life, religious duty and public service were linked in his mind. In old age, replying deprecatingly to a poet's praise of him as one of the immortals, he wrote, "Who are deserving of immortality? They who serve God in truth, and they who have rendered great, essential, and disinterested benefits to their country."

In one of history's most extraordinary examples of planned parenthood, Charles Carroll was called into being by his father to redress injustices to a family and a people. His father sacrificed his young son's happiness and his own pleasures of paternal association to the success of the scheme. The product of this carefully planned conception and rearing grew to love the long-distant father more than he did any other person in the world. When the son himself became a husband and father and was drawn from home by private or public business, he seldom wrote to his wife and son. He habitually wrote to his own father, asking him to relay messages to them.

Not surprisingly, the relationship between Charles Carroll of Carrollton and his son, also named Charles, was not a satisfying one to either party.

Charles Carroll of Carrollton served well his destined role. In his own person, with the aid of contemporary events, he returned his family to the corridors of power, using his influence to bring religious freedom to Maryland and helping to bring it to the nation. In his last years, he was pained by his son's casualness about religion. But he himself, partly because of his reputation for wisdom and virtue and partly because he was the last surviving signer of the Declaration of Independence, the sole living link with the generation of Founding Fathers, was revered as the paterfamilias of a nation. Heartened by his accomplishments but questioning his own selflessness, he relied on the mercy of the Heavenly Father and the intercession of the Son.

12

Haym Salomon

HAYM SALOMON was one of the most important people in the winning of American independence. Yet today his name is known to few Americans.

Why should he be largely forgotten? One factor undoubtedly was his membership in an ethnic minority. He was by birth and rearing a Polish Jew. This is the explanation most likely to be embraced in our time by a generation especially aware of the sin of ethnic exclusion. The point is a valid one, but only part of the story. The eye that moves patiently down columns of figures is not nearly so memorable as the eagle eye that surveys marching columns of uniformed soldiers. Nor is the silent task of computation as dramatic as the fiery oratory that sends men into battle. Thus, even Robert Morris, the Philadelphia financier whose resourcefulness repeatedly rescued the armies and government of the infant republic and whose ethnic profile matched the American norm of his day, is still only a shadowy figure among the Founding Fathers. Those who served by floating bonds are not nearly so well remembered as those who served on ships afloat.

Salomon's greatest contributions were through Robert Morris. But this fact subtracts nothing from Salomon's accomplishments. It is also true that the immigrant Polish Jew made possible some of Morris's most important achievements.

Salomon was almost penniless on arrival in America in 1772 at the age of thirty-two. But the little man brought a wealth of knowledge gleaned in travels in almost every country of his native continent. New York was a thriving port at the time of his arrival, but it is almost certain that none of its residents could match the newcomer's sophisticated knowledge of European currencies. Besides this asset, he also was fluent in Polish, French, Russian, and English.

Growing up in Poland and wandering through Europe, he had seen far too much of tyranny. Soon after arriving in New York City, he joined the Sons of Liberty, originally a secret organization formed in the American colonies to oppose the Stamp Act of 1765. The Sons was often described as a radical group, but, as the Stamp Act was a British revenue measure requiring the use of validating stamps on a host of commercial and legal documents, its ranks soon included many influential citizens. Among these were merchants, other businessmen, lawyers, and journalists. Thus Salomon quickly became known to many of these as a spirited colonial patriot.

His reputation for financial acuity grew with equal rapidity. The poor immigrant rapidly became a prosperous businessman, and the comforts of his home reflected his status. It sheltered not only himself, his wife Rebecca, and the first of their four children but also a series of strangers. These nonpaying guests were colonists whose activities in behalf of freedom had made them fugitives from royal justice. Heavily under suspicion, Salomon was arrested early in the Revolution by his Majesty's officers occupying New York, but won release. He was arrested again, however, in 1778 and suffered a lengthy imprisonment that permanently injured his lungs. He was formally charged with a specific act of treason: while acting as interpreter for the British officers communicating with their Hessian allies, he had persuaded many of the German soldiers to desert. He was convicted and his execution was already scheduled when he contrived to escape and flee to Philadelphia.

The city was then the seat of the confederation under which former colonies, stretching from New England to Georgia, waged war against the mightiest empire on Earth. But even more impressive to Salomon than the town's political significance was its commercial potential. With a population of nearly thirty thousand, it was not only the metropolis of America but second only to London among the most populous cities of the English-speaking world. Many ships under foreign flags crowded its bustling wharves. Here a shrewd and knowledgeable broker, with sufficient nerve, could build a fortune and help the new nation and the cause of freedom at the same time.

Arranging for his family to join him in Philadelphia, Salomon began life anew. His extraordinary brokerage skills, unusual linguistic advantages, proven patriotism, and strong reputation for honesty soon moved him ahead of most business competitors. One of these was Robert Morris. Not always without conflict of interest, Morris was simultaneously one of Philadelphia's leading brokers and the chairman or dominant force in various committees of the Continental Congress through which he was the major agent in coordinating operations of the Revolutionary government. Fortunately, in the final analysis, his patriotism was much stronger than greed. It is unlikely that American independence could have become a reality without him.

Many times the demand for loans to pay long-suffering American troops or to support French aid for the fledgling American government exceeded Morris's resources. Increasingly, after some hesitation, he relied on Salomon. And Salomon repeatedly rose to the need, even when his own financial security was imperiled. The long hours that he labored to make good on his promise further weakened the lungs that had been permanently damaged during his imprisonment. He was literally giving his life to make possible a free society.

A most devoted but realistic patriot, Salomon entertained no notion that he should forsake all Old World institutions to which he had given allegiance. Foremost among these was his Jewish faith. But his old religious values were no impediment to his new life. They were bound up with his patriotic enthusiasm. A devout Jew, imbued with the Polish Jew's hatred of tyranny, he became one of the Philadelphia synagogue's most active members.

When he first came to the city, the congregation of Mickvé Israel, too poor to own a temple, worshiped in a rented room in Stirling Alley. In 1784, Salomon called upon his fellow worshipers to raise a building fund and offered to "bear one fourth of the expense, whatever it might be." The resulting brick temple was the first Jewish house of worship in the city.

Charles Edward Russell, one of the Salomon biographers, has written, "Salomon was most meticulous in the performance of his religious duties." There seems to be no quibbling about that evaluation, but it gives only a partial idea of the scope of religion in his life.

There is a question of motivation. At great personal risk, he assumed debts for the new nation so large that they almost carried him under as a victim of the great economic undertow. He continued in the difficult period after the Americans triumphed at Yorktown in 1781 but did not know until 1783 whether England would renew the fight with its erstwhile colonies or depend on economic disaster to drown them. He personally advanced substantial sums to congressmen so that they might continue to serve the fragile government that could no longer pay them. At least one of them, James Madison, called him "the good Samaritan." The helpfulness of these actions is indisputable. But it might be argued that these generous actions bought him friendships with the influential and might not be an expression of tender concern for his fellow creatures. This suggestion, however, is refuted by another activity of Salomon's in 1783, the same year when he launched the building fund for a synagogue. Simultaneously, as Russell reports, "he was instrumental in founding and furthering a society whose object was to befriend strangers in Philadelphia, no matter what their creed or race." At his own expense, he also helped to feed British soldiers in American prisons.

Devout as he was, Salomon was likely to bend the formal requirements of his faith to serve its humanitarian objectives. There is a story, strongly supported by anecdotal evidence, that he once violated the letter of Jewish law to serve the cause of freedom that he believed sacred. It was Yom Kippur, a holy day when financial transactions were forbidden. A messenger from Robert Morris came to the door of the synagogue while a worship service was in progress. Funds were needed immediately to keep Washington's army in the field. While Morris's man waited, Salomon solicited the congregation and, personally adding to their contributions, provided the necessary thousands of dollars.

But by no means was he ready always to subordinate the welfare of his sect to the demands of government. On January 21, 1784, Salomon was one of five signers, and thought by some people to be the chief promoter, of a petition addressed to the Pennsylvania Council of Censors. Authorized by the constitution of Pennsylvania, the Council was charged with the responsibility of achieving conformity in the operation of state government. The signers wrote that they petitioned "in behalf of themselves and their brethren Jews residing in Pennsylvania." They protested the state constitution's requirement that "each member of the General Assembly of representatives of the foremen of Pennsylvania, before he takes his seat, shall make and subscribe a declaration which ends in these words, 'I do acknowledge the Scriptures of the old and new Testament to be given by divine inspiration.'"

The petitioners protested that this statement conflicted with another constitutional provision, "that no man who acknowledges the being of a God can be justly deprived or abridged of any civil right as a citizen on account of his religious sentiments." Whatever their personal views, Salomon and his fellow petitioners did not protest the exclusion of atheists from the legislative process. But concerning the rule that eligibility would depend partly on the individual's declaration of faith in the divine inspiration of the New Testament, they wrote, "Certainly this religious test deprives the Jews of the most eminent rights of freemen, solemnly ascertained [sic] to all men who are not professed Atheists."

The justice of the petition was officially acknowledged. Years would pass before the civil rights of atheists were fully recognized, but all persons professing a faith in God, be they Christian, Jewish, or adherents of some other religion, organized or individual, were placed on an equal footing in Pennsylvania.

Salomon's physical health continued to decline, but his hopes for his country rose as a peace treaty between Great Britain and America was signed in 1783. There was encouragement in the general vigilance in behalf of liberty and in the fact that congressmen whom he had learned to trust in personal dealings in Philadelphia seemed to be moving toward increased responsibilities.

With the Americans now safely in control of New York City, Salomon foresaw a great future for the city he had had to flee. There was a good chance that it would replace Philadelphia as the American metropolis. He envisioned it as the great brokerage center of the nation, a financial capital of international importance. He had become a poor man in the service of his country, but in New York, if he lived long enough, he could become wealthy again. So he and his family moved back, and he formed a new brokerage partnership. He gave much thought to the location of his office and set it up in a thoroughfare that he expected to become a well-known financial address—Wall Street.

But he was too debilitated to start over in New York. He returned to Philadelphia, and there in January 1785 he died. The strong republic of which he had dreamed, and which his sacrifice helped to make possible, was not yet a reality. But Salomon had seen it coming. Like Moses, he had not lived to be a citizen of the promised land, but he had seen it from afar.

Salomon was as truly a martyr for American independence as any man who died on the battlefield or at sea. He deserves to be far better remembered than he is, not only in justice to his own sacrifices and achievements but also as a reminder of the Revolutionary contributions of other Jews.

Their services were numerous. In Georgia, three Sheftall brothers—David, Levy, and Emanuel—were conspicuous for gallantry on the battlefield. Emanuel escaped just before his scheduled execution by a British firing squad and lived to become the sixth governor of the state of Georgia and apparently the first Jewish chief executive of any American state. Major Benjamin Nones served on the staffs of Washington and Lafayette and was cited for gallantry under Pulaski. Solomon Pinto, an officer in the Connecticut line, was one of the original members of the Society of the Cincinnati in that state. In New York, Pennsylvania, South Carolina, Massachusetts, and Virginia, other Jews were commended for their bravery and unselfish material sacrifice in the American cause. Sometimes it seemed that being a Jew was in itself sufficient reason for the British to suspect a man of pro-American activity.

But few Americans, of his own or any other ethnic background, contributed as much as Haym Salomon to American independence. In none were the passions of piety and patriotism more inextricably blended.

We know tantalizingly little about Salomon's personal faith. But he was a loyal son of Abraham playing a powerful part in the success of the American Revolution. As a dedicated Jew operating within the context of a new nation's struggle for independence, he served well both the rights of Judaism and the cause of universal freedom. Physically small, but large in mind and great in spirit, he was uniquely qualified for his chosen role.

13

What Most People Thought

No one should be surprised that, in America's Revolutionary and early national periods, a laborer and a tradesman, or two small farmers, arguing about religion should come to blows. Then as now, religion, like politics, was an explosive topic. But no one should assume that the trouble started when one accused the other of deviation from Deism. Most Americans seldom wrinkled their brows over the questions of Enlightenment theology passionately pursued by John Adams, Thomas Jefferson, James Madison, and Benjamin Franklin.

Even successful merchants and prosperous country squires, not to mention many highly respected physicians and attorneys, people whose libraries sometimes included classics of literature and history, seldom dove deeply into the murky waters of Deism. Nor did they explore the cloudy heights of metaphysics. They left such decisions of theology and philosophy to the eminent thinkers who dominated their political life, constituting as well an unofficial electoral college of matters spiritual. They would not trouble too much about the arcane speculations of James Madison, John Adams, or John Marshall as long as those gentlemen could be seen in their customary pews on Sunday.

But there were many other Americans, mostly lacking even superficial relationships with the Founding Fathers, who were excitedly following other religious initiatives. The lives of many of these people were being transformed by the Great Awakening. This was a grand-scale Christian revivalist movement that swept through the American colonies in the pre-Revolutionary era, soon losing momentum in New England but gathering force elsewhere in the course of the war, during the establishment of a constitutional national government and in decades that followed. Methodism, which began as a Sunday school movement in the Episcopal Church, became a church in its own right. From the Presbyterian Church sprang separate factions claiming the name Presbyterian. Baptists multiplied, their goal whetted rather than diminished by persecution in some areas. Great outdoor mass meetings were held for worshipers claiming any of a dozen factional allegiances. Some were addressed by gifted orators such as George Whitefield, whose abilities won Benjamin Franklin's admiration. Many preachers were unpolished speakers whose vigorous gestures and shouted messages found eager audiences, especially in the remoter settlements. Even Abraham Lincoln, a genius and a master of language but a true product of the frontier, fondly recalled the evangelists of his youth, saying, "I like for a man to preach like bees are after him."

The flourishing of new sects drew increasing numbers of people away from the Anglican Church, or Episcopal denomination, as it came to be known in America. This severed one more link with England and increased sentiment for independence at the same time that the Founding Fathers concluded that separate nationhood was necessary.

Those drawn by the Great Awakening were not all from a single social stratum. The advocacy of change and the talk of an approaching millennium in fulfillment of the biblical prophecy of a kingdom of justice—these things were extremely attractive to those not satisfied with the status quo. But while many advocates of change were drawn from those who had seldom played a decisive role in government, there were a few influenced by an amalgam of Christian faith and the Enlightenment dream of an ideal republic. Thus Jonathan Edwards, one of New England's intellectual giants, was also a leader of the movement. Samuel Davies, leader of the Virginia Presbyterians, succeeded Edwards as president of Princeton. And there were pockets of religious excitement that included people of social, economic, and political prestige. The Old Dominion's Northern Neck, sometimes called the "Athens of Virginia," numbered among its Baptist congregants Councillor Robert Carter of Nomini Hall and Hannah Lee Corbin. Carter, besides being a powerful man in his own right, was the grandson of the fabulous Robert (King) Carter, richest man in Virginia, rector of the College of William and Mary, and acting governor of the Colony. The younger Carter was so zealous that he provided scholarships for the training of Baptist ministers. Hannah Corbin was the sister of Richard Henry Lee, signer of the Declaration of Independence and president of the Continental Congress.

The aristocratic leavening in dissenting groups sometimes produced friendships between those who had inherited the mantle of leadership and others who had the requisite ability without the opportunity. Besides, plain men of natural gifts sometimes learned through their church work the arts of oratory and leadership. Such people directly influenced both Thomas Jefferson and James Madison in those Founding Fathers' successful labors for religious freedom.

When ratifying conventions met in individual states in 1787 and 1788 to approve or reject the Constitution of the United States submitted by the giants who had met in Philadelphia under the chairmanship of George Washington, many of the delegates were non-Anglicans. They worked side by side with, and sometimes against, men of national reputation. They had the confidence of conviction and in some cases the inspiration of the belief that, in laboring to build the new republic, they were serving the kingdom of God. Some had obtained formal educations at reputable institutions, and some were self-taught in the Bible and the statute books—or, as some of them would have said, in the laws of God and men.

Rarely were these so-called new men deeply versed in the classical history, literature, and philosophy which Adams, Jefferson, Madison, Franklin, and sometimes Washington cited even in informal correspondence. But the ancient texts which they studied reminded them that "the heavens declare the glory of God." And they drew inspiration from one particular star that wise men had begun following long ago.

Some would call their reasoning less sophisticated than that of men who shine most brightly in the constellation of Founding Fathers. Interestingly enough, however, the ruminations of the two groups more often than not led them to support similar measures.

Moreover, the influence of the two was sometimes mutual. This fact is not evident so much in direct individual associations between history's titans among the Founding Fathers and their counterparts among the "new men." It is more obvious in relations between the "new men" and enlightened leaders of statewide reputation to whom the titans listened attentively. Witness the example of Dr. John Tankard, one of Virginia's most distinguished physicians, a product of the old aristocracy, classically educated in Williamsburg and at Edinburgh, then called the world's greatest university. Tankard was a campaign speaker for James Madison. When the Great Awakening was spreading over Virginia, the doctor made an eloquent speech of opposition. He declared,

> I rise to support the dignity of our Church, the old church of our fathers. I rise to support the dignity of men. . . . I shall address your reason, and not your passions. If I can, by plain talk, stop the limit of Folly and Enthusiasm, if I can bring my deluded fellow citizens to their senses, I shall be satisfied. . . . Now, my friends, assist me in supporting our tottering church, or the storms of enthusiasm, which beat so violently against it, will tumble it down. Religion, my friends, is tranquil, does not rant, does not rave, but like the sequestered steam goes smoothly on. Sheltered by the rocks of virtue— unagitated, undisturbed—it gently glides into the great ocean of Eternity.

Before his death, Tankard was using his eloquence in support of a populist Democrat, Andrew Jackson. And when the old physician was gathered to his fathers, the funeral service was a Methodist ceremony.

Few major figures among America's Founding Fathers led "the unexamined life" that Aristotle declared was "not worth living." Whether Protestant, Catholic, or Jewish in faith, liberal or conservative in politics, they perpetually reexamined their lives in the light of ancient wisdom, religious and philosophical. They weighed their actions on a scale of ethics.

Perhaps that is why they earned a remarkable tribute from Alfred North Whitehead, the Englishman who was one of the twentieth century's greatest mathematicians and also one of its greatest philosophers. He said,

> I know of only two occasions in history when the people in power did what needed to be done about as well as you can imagine its being possible. One was the framing of your American Constitution. They were able statesmen; they had access to a body of good ideas; they incorporated these general principles into the instrument without trying to particularize too explicitly how they should be put into effect; and they were men of immense practical experience themselves. The other was in Rome and it undoubtedly saved civilization for, roughly, four hundred years. It was the work of Augustus and the set around him.

The Founding Fathers' habitual rumination on ethics, no less than their inspired pursuit of wisdom, may have had a good deal to do with the greatness of their era. Of course, they did not *always* live up to their ideals. People who do have low standards.

Appendix

VIRGINIA STATUTE FOR
RELIGIOUS FREEDOM

Passed as a Statute by the Virginia General Assembly in January 1786

WHEREAS Almighty God hath created the mind free; that all attempts to influence it by temporal punishments or burthens, or by civil incapacitations, tend only to beget habits of hypocrisy and meanness, and are a departure from the plan of the Holy author of our religion, who being Lord both of body and mind, yet chose not to propagate it by coercions on either, as it was in his Almighty power to do; that the impious presumption of legislators and rulers, civil as well as ecclesiastical, who being themselves but fallible and uninspired men, have assumed dominion over the faith of others, setting up their own opinions and modes of thinking as the only true and infallible, and as such endeavouring to impose them on others, hath established and maintained false religions over the greatest part of the world, and through all time; that to compel a man to furnish contributions of money for the propagation of opinions which he disbelieves, is sinful and tyrannical; that even forcing him to support this or that teacher of his own religious persuasion, is depriving him of the comfortable liberty of giving his contributions to the particular pastor, whose morals he would make his pattern, and whose powers he feels most persuasive to righteousness, and is withdrawing from the ministry those temporary rewards, which proceeding from an approbation of their personal conduct,

are an additional incitement to earnest and unremitting labours for
the instruction of mankind; that our civil rights have no dependence on our religious opinions, any more than our opinions in
physics or geometry; that therefore the proscribing any citizen as
unworthy of the public confidence by laying upon him an incapac-
ity of being called to offices of trust and emolument, unless he profess or renounce this or that religious opinion, is depriving him in-
juriously of those privileges and advantages to which in common
with his fellow-citizens he has a natural right; that it tends only to
corrupt the principles of that religion it is meant to encourage, by
bribing with a monopoly of worldly honours and emoluments,
those who will externally profess and conform to it; that though indeed these are criminal who do not withstand such temptation, yet
neither are those innocent who lay the bait in their way; that to suffer the civil magistrate to intrude his powers into the field of opinion, and to restrain the profession or propagation of principles on
supposition of their ill tendency, is a dangerous fallacy, which at
once destroys all religious liberty, because he being of course judge
of that tendency will make his opinions the rule of judgment, and
approve or condemn the sentiments of others only as they shall
square with or differ from his own; that it is time enough for the
rightful purposes of civil government, for its officers to interfere
when principles break out into overt acts against peace and good
order; and finally, that truth is great and will prevail if left to herself, that she is the proper and sufficient antagonist to error, and has
nothing to fear from the conflict, unless by human interposition
disarmed of her natural weapons, free argument and debate, errors
ceasing to be dangerous when it is permitted freely to contradict
them:

BE IT ENACTED by the General Assembly, That no man shall
be compelled to frequent or support any religious worship, place,
or ministry whatsoever, nor shall be enforced, restrained, molested,
or burthened in his body or goods, nor shall otherwise suffer on account of his religious opinions or belief; but that all men shall be

free to profess, and by argument to maintain, their opinion in matters of religion, and that the same shall in no wise diminish enlarge, or affect their civil capacities.

AND THOUGH we well know that this assembly elected by the people for the ordinary purposes of legislation only, have no power to restrain the acts of succeeding assemblies, constituted with powers equal to our own, and that therefore to declare this act to be irrevocable would be of no effect in law; yet we are free to declare, and do declare, that the rights hereby asserted are of the natural rights of mankind, and that if any act shall be hereafter passed to repeal the present, or to narrow its operation, such act shall be an infringement of natural right.

Bibliography

I used few theological works in researching for this book. I am not a theologian. But neither were any of the Founding Fathers I have discussed, with the possible exception of James Madison, who studied the subject at Princeton under Rev. John Witherspoon, and Charles Carroll, who was tutored in it by a succession of Jesuit priests. John Adams was an earnest reader of works on Christianity, Greek and Roman religions, and the Hindu faith. I have called Thomas Jefferson a "closet theologian," since he pursued most of his theological ruminations in secrecy; but few professional theologians would concede the designation.

This book is mostly concerned with the thoughts on religion of intelligent political leaders prominent in the founding of the United States. Some were geniuses. None was stupid. Their ideas on the subject are valuable chiefly as evidence of the philosophies and inspirations of a remarkable group of nation builders. They may be of special interest to those bewildered by writers and speakers who, in the service of conscious or unconscious agendas, have presented the Founding Fathers as uniformly secret atheists or hard-rock fundamentalists.

A great variety of sources was useful to me in re-creating the religious milieu of the Founding Fathers. They may well be helpful to readers of this book who would like to explore a little for themselves.

GENERAL

Ahlstrom, Sidney E. *A Religious History of the American People*. New Haven, 1972. Though only chapter 23 (pp. 360–384) of this 1,158-page book deals directly with the Revolutionary Era, the work as a whole illuminates both antecedent and resulting movements in American religious culture.

Bonomi, Patricia U. *Under the Cope of Heaven: Religion, Society, and Politics in Colonial America*. New York, 1986.

Bridenbaugh, Carl. *Mitre and Sceptre: Transatlantic Faiths, Ideas, Personalities, and Politics, 1689–1775*. New York, 1962.

Commager, Henry Steele. *The Empire of Reason: How Europe Imagined and America Realized the Enlightenment*. Garden City, N. Y., 1977.

Cousins, Norman. *In God We Trust: The Religious Beliefs and Ideas of the Founding Fathers*. New York, 1958.

Davis, Richard Beale. *Intellectual Life in the Colonial South, 1585–1763*. Knoxville, Tenn. 1978.

Gaustad, Edwin S. *Faith of Our Fathers: Religion and the New Nation*. San Francisco, 1987.

———. *Neither King nor Prelate: Religion and the New Nation, 1776–1826*. Grand Rapids, Mich., 1993. Emphasizes variety of religious opinions in the half century.

Heimert, Alan E. *Religion and the American Mind from the Great Awakening to the Revolution*. Cambridge, Mass., 1966. Detailed.

Hoffman, Ronald, and Peter J. Albert, eds. *Religion in a Revolutionary Age*. Charlottesville, Va., 1994. Especially the following essays: Patricia U. Bonomi, "Religious Dissent and the Case for American Exceptionalism," pp. 31–51; Ronald Schultz, "God and Workingmen," pp. 125–155; Stephen A. Martin, "Religion, Politics and Ratification," pp. 184–217; and Paul K. Conkin, "Priestley and Jefferson: Unitarianism as a Religion for a New Revolutionary Age," pp. 290–307.

Koch, Adrienne. *Power, Morals, and the Founding Fathers: Essays in the Interpretation of the American Enlightenment*. Ithaca, N.Y., 1961. Particularly useful on Benjamin Franklin, Thomas Jefferson, and James Madison.

Koch, G. Adolph. *Republican Religion: The American Revolution and the Cult of Reason*. Gloucester, Mass., 1964.

May, Henry F. *The Enlightenment in America*. New York, 1976. On first publication, this book was hailed by distinguished scholars as "the most comprehensive survey of the topic." It is still one of the most useful and certainly one of the most readable.

Sweet, William Warren. *Religion in the Development of American Culture, 1765–1840*. New York, 1952. Clear and informative.

Weisberger, Bernard A. *America Afire: Jefferson, Adams, and the Revolutionary Election of 1800*. New York, 2000.

Wood, Gordon S. *The Creation of the American Republic, 1776–1787*. Chapel Hill, N.C., 1969. This volume is helpful in acquiring an understanding of the milieu that produced the Founding Fathers.

BIBLIOGRAPHY

Some sources have provided important information and insights connected with the character and religious beliefs of individuals discussed in the separate chapters. Professional scholars and other serious researchers can find scholarly magazine references in parenthesized citations in the main text. Quotations from the letters of historical figures, whether available in books or in Library of Congress or other microfilm, can be found readily with the aid of names and dates provided in the main text.

CHAPTER 2: THOMAS JEFFERSON

Jefferson's own writings are the most important sources. Among the most significant in connection with the subject of this book are:

Cappon, Lester J., ed. *The Adams–Jefferson Letters: The Complete Correspondence between Thomas Jefferson and John and Abigail Adams.* Chapel Hill, N.C., 1959. With few people did Jefferson share his religious views as freely as with John Adams.

Cullen, Charles T., ed. *The Papers of Thomas Jefferson*, second series, *Jefferson's Extracts from the Gospel*, ed. Charles T. Cullen. Princeton, N.J., 1983.

Dreisbach, Daniel L. *Thomas Jefferson and the Wall of Separation between Church and State.* New York, 2002. A compact masterpiece of thorough research and insightful interpretation.

Jefferson, Thomas. *Virginia Statute for Religious Freedom.* Appendix in this volume.

Other significant sources dealing with Jefferson's religion are:

Bailyn, Bernard, ed. *The Debate on the Constitution*, 2 vols. New York, 1993. The able editor of this collection is one of America's most honored historians.

Bowers, Claude. *Civil and Religious Liberty: Jefferson.* Worcester, Mass., 1930.

Cousins, Norman. *In God We Trust: The Religious Beliefs and Ideas of the American Founding Fathers.* New York, 1958.

Foote, Henry Wilder. *Thomas Jefferson: Champion of Religious Freedom, Advocate of Christian Morals.* Boston, 1997.

Gaustad, Edwin S. *Sworn Upon the Altar of God: A Religious Biography of Thomas Jefferson.* Grand Rapids, Mich., 1996.

Gould, William D. "The Religious Opinions of Thomas Jefferson." *The Mississippi Valley Historical Review* 20 (1935): 191–208.

Hall, Leslie. "The Religious Opinions of Thomas Jefferson." *Sewanee Review* 21 (1913): 164–176.

Roche, O. I. A. *The Jefferson Bible, with the Annotated Commentaries on Religion of Thomas Jefferson.* New York, 1964.

Sanford, Charles B. *The Religious Life of Thomas Jefferson.* Charlottesville, Va.., 1984.

Schultz, Constance Bartlett. "The Radical Religious Ideas of Thomas Jefferson and John Adams: A Comparison." Ph.D. Diss., University of Cincinnati, 1973.

Sheldon, Garrett Ward, and Daniel L. Dreisbach. *Religion and Political Culture in Jefferson's Virginia.* Lanham, Md., 2000.

White, Morton. *The Philosophy of the American Revolution.* New York, 1978. Morton White, chairman of the Department of Philosophy at Harvard University and also a professor of the Institute for Advanced Study in Princeton, is one of America's foremost historians of ideas. This brief book is a stimulating and provocative discussion of intellectual concepts that may have influenced the political and religious views of some of the Founding Fathers. Particularly interesting in regard to Jefferson is Professor White's exposition of the Virginian's evolving views on reason in morals, p. 114–127, and on the moral ends of government, pp. 253–254. Also helpful is chapter 4, "The Laws of Nature and of Nature's God," pp. 142–184.

Wood, Gordon S. *The Creation of the American Republic, 1776–1787.* Chapel Hill, N.C., 1969. This volume is helpful in acquiring an understanding of the milieu that produced the Founding Fathers.

More general works on Jefferson are:

Malone, Dumas. *Jefferson and His Time,* 6 vols. Boston, 1948.

Mapp, Alf J., Jr., *Thomas Jefferson: A Strange Case of Mistaken Identity.* Lanham, Md., 1987. Carries Jefferson from birth to his inauguration as president.

———. *Thomas Jefferson: Passionate Pilgrim.* Lanham, Md., 1991. Carries Jefferson through both terms as president to the founding of the University of Virginia and his death. Both Mapp volumes treat the human side of Jefferson as well as his public career.

Peterson, Merrill D., and Robert C. Vaughan. *The Virginia Statute for Religious Freedom: Its Evolution and Consequences in American History.* Cambridge, England, 1988. Particularly interesting is chapter 4, "The Political Theology of Thomas Jefferson," by Thomas E. Buckley, S.J., in which he argues that "Jefferson's case for liberty of belief and expression anticipates statements from [our] contemporary Christian bodies, such as the World Council of Churches and the Second Vatican Council."

Preston, Daniel. *A Comprehensive Catalogue of the Correspondence and Papers of James Monroe,* vols. 1 and 2. Westport, Conn., 2001. Because of Monroe's long association with Jefferson, this superbly edited catalog, containing approximately 35,800 entries, is extremely valuable to serious Jefferson scholars.

Those interested in extensive research on Jefferson may wish to consult the seven-page bibliography in Alf J. Mapp, Jr., *Thomas Jefferson: A Strange Case of Mistaken Identity*, and the six-page bibliography in Alf J. Mapp, Jr., *Thomas Jefferson: Passionate Pilgrim*. These bibliographies include manuscript and microfilm sources as well as printed materials.

CHAPTER 3: BENJAMIN FRANKLIN

Information on Franklin is derived primarily from the following sources:

Adams, Charles Francis, ed. *The Works of John Adams, Second President of the United States: With a Life of the Author, Notes, and Illustrations*. Boston, 1856.

Aldridge, Alfred Owen. *Benjamin Franklin and Nature's God*. Durham, N.C., 1967.

———. *Benjamin Franklin: Philosopher and Man*. Philadelphia, 1965.

———. *Franklin and His French Contemporaries*. New York, 1957.

Anderson, Douglas. *The Radical Enlightenments of Benjamin Franklin*. Baltimore, 1997.

Bailyn, Bernard, ed. *The Debate on the Constitution*, 2 vols. New York, 1993. The able editor of this collection is one of America's most honored historians. Particularly pertinent is Franklin's speech in Philadelphia on September 17, 1787, vol. 1, pp. 3–5. Also of interest are his references to "the great designer of providence," vol. 1, pp. 867–868.

Best, John Hardin. *Benjamin Franklin on Education*. New York, 1962.

Brands, H. W. *The First American: The Life and Times of Benjamin Franklin*. New York, 2000. Readable and perceptive. Perhaps the best biography of Franklin yet published.

Burlingame, Roger. *Benjamin Franklin: Envoy Extraordinary*. New York, 1967.

Cohen, I. Bernard. *Benjamin Franklin: Scientist and Statesman*. New York, 1975.

———. *Science and the Founding Fathers: Science in the Political Thought of Jefferson, Adams, Franklin, and Madison*. New York, 1995.

Cohen, I. Bernard, ed. *Benjamin Franklin's Experiments: A New Edition of Franklin's "Experiments and Observations on Electricity."* Cambridge, Mass., 1941.

Crane, Verner W. *Benjamin Franklin and a Rising People*. Boston, 1954.

Currey, Cecil B. *Road to Revolution: Benjamin Franklin in England, 1765–1775*. Garden City, N.Y., 1968.

Farrand, Max. *Benjamin Franklin's Memoirs*. Cambridge, Mass., 1936, reprinted for private circulation by the *Huntington Library Bulletin*, no. 10 (October 1936).

Fleming, Thomas J. *The Man Who Dared the Lightning: A New Look at Benjamin Franklin*. New York, 1971.

BIBLIOGRAPHY

Ford, Paul Leicester. *The Many-Sided Franklin*. 1898. Reprint, Freeport, N.Y., 1972.
Granger, Bruce Ingham. *Benjamin Franklin: An American Man of Letters*. Ithaca, N.Y., 1964.
Lopez, Claude-Anne. *Mon Cher Papa: Franklin and the Ladies of Paris*. New Haven, Conn., 1966.
Mapp, Alf J., Jr., *Three Golden Ages: Discovering the Creative Secrets of Renaissance Florence, Elizabethan England, and America's Founding*. Lanham, Md., 1998. Chapter 29, "The Philadelphia Wizard," pp. 353–362.
Middlekauff, Robert. *Benjamin Franklin and His Enemies*. Berkeley, Calif., 1996.
Miles, Richard D. "The American Image of Benjamin Franklin," *American Quarterly* 9 (Summer 1957): 117–143.
Morgan, David T. *The Devious Dr. Franklin, Colonial Agent*. Macon, Ga., 1996.
Smyth, Albert Henry, ed. *The Writings of Benjamin Franklin*, vol. 1. New York, 1905.
Tully, Alan. *Forming American Politics: Ideas, Interests, and Institutions in Colonial New York and Pennsylvania*. Baltimore, 1994, p. 200. The friend was John Hughes, leader of the Quaker Party. Franklin's own newspaper refused to print his recommendation that Hughes be appointed.
Van Doren, Carl. *Benjamin Franklin*. New York, 1938.
Van Doren, Carl, ed. *Benjamin Franklin and Jonathan Edwards: Selections from Their Writings*. New York, 1920.
Winegard, Dilys P. *The Intellectual World of Benjamin Franklin*. Philadelphia, 1990.
Wood, Gordon S. *The Creation of the American Republic, 1776–1787*. Chapel Hill, N.C., 1969. This volume is helpful in acquiring an understanding of the milieu that produced the Founding Fathers.
Woody, Thomas, ed. *Educational Views of Benjamin Franklin*. New York, 1971.

CHAPTER 4: JAMES MADISON

Adams, Henry. *History of the United States during the Administrations of Jefferson and Madison*. 9 vols. New York, 1891–1893.
Banning, Lance. *The Sacred Fire of Liberty: James Madison and the Founding of the Federal Republic*. Ithaca, N.Y., 1995.
Bemis, Samuel Flagg, ed.. *The American Secretaries of State and Their Diplomacy*, vol. 3. New York, 1958.
Brant, Irving. *James Madison: The Virginia Revolutionist, 1751–1780*, James Madison Series, vol. 1. Indianapolis, 1941.
———. *James Madison: The Nationalist, 1780–1787*, James Madison Series, vol. 2. Indianapolis, 1948.
———. *James Madison: Father of the Constitution, 1787–1800*, James Madison Series, vol. 3. Indianapolis, 1950.

BIBLIOGRAPHY

———. *James Madison: Secretary of State, 1800–1809*, James Madison Series, vol. 4. Indianapolis, 1953.

———. *James Madison: The President, 1809–1812*, James Madison Series, vol. 5. Indianapolis, 1956.

———. *James Madison: Commander-in-Chief, 1812–1836*, James Madison Series, vol. 6. Indianapolis, 1961.

Brugger, Robert J., et al., eds. *The Papers of James Madison*: Secretary of State Series, 3 vols. Charlottesville, Va., 1986.

Burnett, Edmund C., ed., *Letters of Members of the Continental Congress*, 8 vols., 1921. Reprint, Gloucester, Mass., 1963.

Gay, Sydney Howard. *James Madison*. Boston, 1898.

Grigsby, Hugh Blair. *The History of the Virginia Federal Convention of 1788*, ed. R. A. Brock, 2 vols. Richmond, Va., 1890–1891.

Hunt, Gaillard. *The Life of James Madison*. New York, 1902.

———. *The Writings of James Madison*, 9 vols. New York, 1900–1910.

Hunt, Gaillard, and James B. Scott, eds. *Journal of the Federal Convention, The Debates in the Federal Convention of 1787*. Westport, Conn., 1970.

Hunt-Jones, Conover. *Dolley and "the Great Little Madison."* AIA Foundation, Washington, D.C., 1977.

Hutchinson, William T., William M. E. Rachal, and Robert A. Rutland, eds. *The Papers of James Madison*, 15 vols. Chicago, 1962–1985.

Jefferson, Thomas. *The Papers of Thomas Jefferson*, ed. Julian P. Boyd, L. H. Butterfield, and Charles T. Cullen, 25 vols. Princeton, N.J., 1950–1992.

———. *The Republic of Letters: The Correspondence between Thomas Jefferson and James Madison, 1776–1826*, ed. James Morton Smith, 3 vols. New York, 1995.

Koch, Adrienne. *Jefferson and Madison: The Great Collaboration*. New York, 1950.

Koch, Adrienne, and Harry Ammon. "The Virginia and Kentucky Resolutions: An Episode in Jefferson's and Madison's Defense of Civil Liberties," *William and Mary Quarterly*, 3d series, 5 April 1968.

Madison, James. James Madison Papers, Presidential Papers, Library of Congress, microfilm, 28 reels (Washington, D.C., 1964), *Letters and Other Writings of James Madison*, published by order of Congress, 4 vols. Philadelphia, 1867.

Madison, James, Alexander Hamilton, and John Jay. *The Federalist*, ed. Benjamin Fletcher Wright. Cambridge, Mass., 1961.

Matthews, Richard K. *If Men Were Angels: James Madison and the Heartless Empire of Reason*. Lawrence, Kans., 1995.

Peterson, Merrill D., ed. *James Madison: A Biography in His Own Words*. New York, 1974.

Preston, Daniel. *A Comprehensive Catalogue of the Correspondence and Papers of James Monroe*, vols. 1 and 2. Westport, Conn., 2001. Because of Monroe's long association with Madison, this superbly edited catalog, containing approximately 35,800 entries, is extremely valuable to serious Madison scholars.

Rakove, Jack N. *James Madison and the Creation of the American Republic*, ed. Oscar Handlin. Glenview, Ill., 1990.

Rives, William C. *History of the Life and Times of James Madison*, 3 vols. Freeport, N.Y., 1970.

Rutland, Robert A. *James Madison: The Founding Father.* New York, 1987.

———. *The Presidency of James Madison.* Lawrence, Kans., 1990.

Rutland, Robert A., ed. *James Madison and the American Nation, 1751–1836: An Encyclopedia.* New York, 1994.

Rutland, Robert A., et al., eds. *The Papers of James Madison*: Presidential Series, 2 vols. Charlottesville, Va., 1984.

Smith, Margaret Bayard. *The First Forty Years of Washington Society, Portrayed by the Family Letters of Mrs. Samuel Harrison Smith from the Collection of Her Grandson, J. Henly Smith.* New York, 1906.

Wills, Gary. *James Madison.* New York, 2002. Should be read in connection with Irving Brant's *James Madison.* Wills returns to the pre-Brant thesis of Madison as a great thinker and statesman but poor president.

Wood, Gordon S. *The Creation of the American Republic, 1776–1787.* Chapel Hill, N.C., 1969. This volume is helpful in acquiring an understanding of the milieu that produced the Founding Fathers.

CHAPTER 5: JOHN ADAMS

Adams, Charles Francis, ed. *Familiar Letters of John Adams and His Wife Abigail Adams during the Revolution.* New York, 1876. Generally reliable, though occasionally censored by the Victorian hand of a reverential grandson.

———. *The Works of John Adams*, vols. I–X. Boston, 1856.

Adams, James Truslow. *The Adams Family.* Boston, 1930.

Bailyn, Bernard. *Faces of Revolution: Personalities and Themes in the Struggle for American Independence.* New York, 1990, pp. 3–21. The work of a distinguished historian who appreciates John Adams's literary style and captures his personality in less than eighteen pages.

———, ed. *The Debate on the Constitution*, 2 vols. New York, 1993. The able editor of this collection is one of America's most honored historians.

Butterfield, L. H., ed. *Adams Family Correspondence*, vols. I–VI. The Adams Papers. Cambridge, Mass., 1963. Filled with significant facts and enlivened by the pithy frankness of John Adams and Abigail. On June 2, 1776, John wrote Abigail, "I really think that your letters are much better worth preserving than mine" (vol. II, p. 3).

BIBLIOGRAPHY

———, ed. *Diary and Autobiography of John Adams*, vols. I–IV. The Adams Papers. Cambridge, Mass., 1961.

———, ed. *The Earliest Diary of John Adams*. The Adams Papers. Cambridge, Mass., 1966. Covers two periods, June 1753–April 1754 and September 1758–January 1759. Butterfield's introduction, pp. 1–42, is useful for an understanding of young John Adams.

Cappon, Lester J., ed. *The Adams–Jefferson Letters*, 2 vols. Chapel Hill, N.C., 1959. This work, the principal source of communications between Adams and Jefferson, is the source of Adams's important letter of December 8, 1818, declaring his faith in immortality (*The Adams–Jefferson Letters*, vol. 2, p. 530).

Ellis, Joseph J. *Passionate Sage*. New York, 1993.

Ferling, John. *John Adams: A Biography*. Wesport, Conn., 1994.

———. *John Adams: A Life*. Knoxville, Tenn., 1992. An objective, well-researched biography.

McCullough, David. *John Adams*. New York, 2001. Fresh interpretations by an entertaining writer.

Nagel, Paul C. *Descent from Glory: Four Generations of the John Adams Family*. New York, 1983. John Adams in the context of his family and his times. By a historian both scholarly and readable.

———. *The Adams Women: Abigail and Louise Adams*. New York, 1987.

———. *John Quincey Adams: A Public Life, A Private Life*. New York, 1997.

Shaw, Peter. *The Character of John Adams*. New York, 1976. In chapter I, pp. 3–24, Shaw shows the influence of Puritanism on Adams's self-conscious attempt to curb his vanity. In chapter VIII, "The Consolations of Philosophy," the author shows the Bible's moderating influence on Adams's attitude toward Enlightenment ideas of government.

Thompson, C. Bradley. *John Adams and the Spirit of Liberty*. Lawrence, Kans., 1998. Chapter 1, "Calvin, Locke, and the American Enlightenment," pp. 3–23, is helpful to the reader in reconciling elements of Adams's faith that might appear contradictory upon cursory consideration. The author presents Adams's religious philosophy as a combination of Calvinism and the tenets of the Enlightenment. Knowledge came through the senses, and God-given reason evaluated the evidence.

White, Morton. *The Philosophy of the American Revolution*. New York, 1978. Morton White, chairman of the Department of Philosophy at Harvard University and also a professor of the Institute for Advanced Study in Princeton, is one of America's foremost historians of ideas. This brief book is a stimulating and provocative discussion of intellectual concepts that may have influenced the political and religious views of some of the Founding Fathers. Of interest is Professor White's examination of Adams's supposed "utilitarianism," pp. 235–244.

Wood, Gordon S. *The Creation of the American Republic, 1776–1787.* Chapel Hill, N.C., 1969. This volume is helpful in acquiring an understanding of the milieu that produced the Founding Fathers.

CHAPTER 6: GEORGE WASHINGTON

The most detailed biography of Washington is the well-researched and largely objective one by Douglas Southall Freeman, who for this work won his second Pulitzer prize for biography. It consists of six volumes written by Freeman and a seventh completed posthumously by his research assistants.

Bailyn, Bernard, ed. *The Debate on the Constitution*, 2 vols. New York, 1993. The able editor of this collection is one of America's most honored historians.

Boller, Jr., Paul F. *George Washington and Religion.* Dallas, 1963.

Brookhiser, Richard. *Founding Father: Rediscovering George Washington.* New York, 1996. Delightfully written and freshly interpretive. In pages 144–149, Brookhiser discusses Washington's attitude toward Providence, citing some of the quotations used in our chapter.

Freeman, Douglas Southall. *George Washington*, vol. I & II, *Young Washington.* New York, 1948.

———. *George Washington*, vol. III, *Planter and Patriot.* New York, 1948.

———. *George Washington*, vol. IV, *Leader of the Revolution.* New York, 1951.

———. *George Washington*, vol. V, *Victory with the Help of France.* New York, 1952.

———. *George Washington*, vol. VI, *Patriot and President*, New York, 1954.

Freeman, Douglas Southall, John Alexander Carroll, and Mary Wells Ashworth. *George Washington*, vol. VII, *First in Peace.* New York, 1952.

Henriques, Peter R. "The Final Struggle between George Washington and the Grim King." *The Virginia Magazine of History and Biography* 107 (1999): 73–97.

Mayo, Bernard. *Myths and Men: Patrick Henry, George Washington, Thomas Jefferson.* Athens, Ga., 1959. The essays on Henry, Washington, and Jefferson were delivered by Professor Mayo in the Dorothy Blount Lamar Memorial Lecture series at Mercer University, November 19–20, 1958. The chapter on Washington includes instances of his warm humanity, as when he returned to British General Sir William Howe "his little pet dog that had wandered off into no-man's land," p. 45.

Wood, Gordon S. *The Creation of the American Republic, 1776–1787.* Chapel Hill, N.C., 1969. This volume is helpful in acquiring an understanding of the milieu that produced the Founding Fathers.

BIBLIOGRAPHY

Washington's own writings contain many surprises, not only for lay persons, but also for many American historians who have not specialized in his life. These are available in several editions:

Abbott, W. W., Dorothy Twohig, et al. *The Papers of George Washington.* Charlottesville, Va., 1983.
Fitzpatrick, John C., ed. *Writings of George Washington.* 39 vols. Washington, D.C., 1931–1939.

Other significant references are:

Flexner, James Thomas. *George Washington.* 4 vols. Boston, 1965–1972.
Longmore, Paul K. *The Invention of George Washington.* Berkeley, Calif., 1988.

CHAPTER 7: JOHN MARSHALL

Ammon, Harry. "Agricola versus Aristides: James Monroe, John Marshall, and the Genet Affair in Virginia." *Virginia Magazine of History and Bibliography* 71 (1963): 395–418.
Beveridge, Albert J. *The Life of John Marshall,* 4 vols. Boston, 1916.
Davis, Burke. *A Williamsburg Galaxy.* Williamsburg, Va., 1968, p. 212.
Dewey, Donald O. *Marshall versus Jefferson.* New York, 1970.
Haskins, George L. *The Foundations of Power: John Marshall, 1801–1815.* New York, 1981.
Hobson, Charles F. *The Great Chief Justice: John Marshall and the Rule of Law.* Lawrence, Kans., 1996. I have also benefited from discussions with Professor Charles F. Hobson, one of the best of Marshall biographers and editor of *The Papers of John Marshall.*
Johnson, Herbert Alan. "John Marshall." In *The Justices of the United States Supreme Court, 1789–1978: Their Lives and Major Opinions* 1. New York, 1980, pp. 285–351.
Marshall, John. *An Autobiographical Sketch by John Marshall written at the Request of Joseph Story and Now Printed for the First Time from the Original Manuscript Preserved at the William L. Clements Library, Together with a Letter from Chief Justice Marshall to Justice Story Relating Thereto,* ed. John Stokes Adams. Ann Arbor, Mich., 1937.
Mays, David John. *Edmund Pendleton, 1721–1803: A Biography* 1. Cambridge, Mass., 1952, pp. 168–169.
Morpurgo, J. E. *Their Majesties' Royall Colledge.* Williamsburg, Va., 1976, p. 133–134.
Newmyer, R. Kent. *John Marshall and the Heroic Age of the Supreme Court.* Baton Rouge, La., 2001. The book has little to say about Marshall's religious

views per se, but his ethics and the operations of his conscience are discussed, especially in pp. 463–483.

Smith, Jean E. *John Marshall: Definer of a Nation*. New York, 1996.

White, G. Edward. *The Marshall Court and Cultural Change, 1815–1835*. Oxford, 1991.

Wood, Gordon S. *The Creation of the American Republic, 1776–1787*. Chapel Hill, N.C., 1969. This volume is helpful in acquiring an understanding of the milieu that produced the Founding Fathers.

John Marshall's law notes, account books, and other papers in Special Collections (Archives), Earl Gregg Swem Library, College of William and Mary, Williamsburg, Virginia, and *The Papers of John Marshall*, ed. Charles F. Hobson, vols. 1–11. Chapel Hill, N.C., 1974–2002.

CHAPTER 8: PATRICK HENRY

Bailyn, Bernard, ed. *The Debate on the Constitution*, 2 vols. New York, 1993. The able editor of this collection is one of America's most honored historians.

Beeman, Richard R. *Patrick Henry: A Biography*. New York, 1974. Though only 229 pages, by no means superficial. The author's sometimes acerbic skepticism stops short of hostility to the subject and is an antidote to the unchecked adulation of some works. Valuable information on Henry's financial status and acquisitive disposition (some of it condensed from Jackson T. Main, "The One Hundred," *William and Mary Quarterly*, series 3, XI [1954]: 354–384) is provided in pp. 173–184 of Beeman's book.

Henry, William Wirt. *Patrick Henry: Life, Correspondence, and Speeches*, 3 vols., 1891. Reprint, Harrisonburg, Va., 1993. As the work of Henry's grandson, these books lack objectivity but speak with special authority on details of the statesman's personal life.

Mayer, Henry. *A Son of Thunder: Patrick Henry and the American Republic*. New York, 1986. Henry's connection with the religious issues of his day is explored in chapters 7 and 9, especially pp. 157–168 and 358–364, and in the epilogue, where the increasingly religious tone of his last years and days is illustrated with quotations.

Mayo, Bernard. *Myths and Men: Patrick Henry, George Washington, Thomas Jefferson*. Athens, Ga., 1959. The essays on Henry, Washington, and Jefferson were delivered by Professor Mayo in the Dorothy Blount Lamar Memorial Lecture series at Mercer University, November 19–20, 1958. The chapter titled "The Enigma of Patrick Henry," pp. 1–23, alerts the reader to prejudiced judgments in William Wirt's biography of Henry.

Meade, Robert Douthat. *Patrick Henry*, 2 vols. Philadelphia, 1957–69. A work of dependable scholarship.

Morgan, George. *The True Patrick Henry*. Philadelphia, 1907.

BIBLIOGRAPHY

Randolph, Edmund. *History of Virginia*, ed. Arthur Shaffer. Charlottesville, Va., 1970. Perceptive views of Henry by a highly intelligent and fair-minded person who knew him personally. I first used the book in manuscript form (Virginia Historical Society collection), but it has been made even more useful by Shaffer's editing. Of course, as I have indicated in my chapter on Henry, Edmund Randolph mistakenly thought that the orator had sprung from a humble background, a view that Henry himself did not discourage at the beginning of his political career. But Randolph's personal observations are reliable.

Tyler, Moses Coit. *Patrick Henry*. Boston, 1887. Reprint, 1972.

Willison, George. *Patrick Henry and His World*. New York, 1969.

Wood, Gordon S. *The Creation of the American Republic, 1776–1787*. Chapel Hill, N.C., 1969. This volume is helpful in acquiring an understanding of the milieu that produced the Founding Fathers.

CHAPTER 9: ALEXANDER HAMILTON

Bailyn, Bernard, ed. *The Debate on the Constitution*, 2 vols. New York, 1993. The able editor of this collection is one of America's most honored historians.

Broadus, Mitchell. *Alexander Hamilton: Youth to Maturity*. New York, 1957.

———. *Alexander Hamilton: The National Adventurer*. New York, 1962. Both of Broadus's works are detailed and extensively researched.

Brookhiser, Richard. *Alexander Hamilton, American*. New York, 1999. Insightful and entertainingly written.

Cooke, Jacob Ernest. *Alexander Hamilton*. New York, 1982. A brief but scholarly book by the general editor of the first fifteen volumes of *The Papers of Alexander Hamilton*. Some readers may find provocative his use of Freudian and neo-Freudian psychology in analyzing Hamilton's personality.

Ellis, Joseph J. *Founding Brothers: The Revolutionary Generation*. New York, 2000. Chapter One, "The Duel," pp. 20–47, analyzes the possible intentions of Hamilton and Aaron Burr on that occasion.

Miller, John Chester. *Alexander Hamilton and the Growth of the New Nation*. New York, 1959. Integrates Hamilton's life with the nation's political and financial history. There is not a great deal about Hamilton's religion per se, but several observations deserve attention, such as Miller's discussion of the premise that "All that Hamilton asked of British statesmen was that they conduct the affairs of the Empire in conformity with the will of God" and the biographer's observation that "like most American patriots of his generation, Hamilton believed that he was fully competent to elucidate the intentions of the Almighty"; and Miller's own pithy elucidation of a Hamilton quote: "The sacred rights of mankind are not to be rummaged for among old parchments or musty records. They are written, as with a sunbeam, in the whole volume of human nature, by the hand of the Divinity itself, and can never be erased or obscured by mortal power" (pp. 14–15). Related observations are on pp. 50, 121–122, 202–203, and 285.

Schachner, Nathan. *Alexander Hamilton.* New York, 1946. Though good biographies of Hamilton have been published since Schachner's, they have not made his work obsolete. Schachner had both wide learning and common sense.

Syrett, Harold, ed. *The Papers of Alexander Hamilton,* 26 vols. New York, 1961, 1974, 1992. Hamilton's letters are not as revelatory of personality as those of John Adams and Thomas Jefferson and therefore not of as much general interest as theirs, but of course are an essential resource for the professional researcher.

White, Morton. *The Philosophy of the American Revolution.* New York, 1978. Morton White, chairman of the Department of Philosophy at Harvard University and also a professor of the Institute for Advanced Study in Princeton, is one of America's foremost historians of ideas. This brief book is a stimulating and provocative discussion of intellectual concepts that may have influenced the political and religious views of some of the Founding Fathers. Of interest is Professor White's examination of Hamilton's concept of self-evident truths as "written in the whole volume of human nature by the hand of the divinity itself," pp. 78–96.

Wood, Gordon S. *The Creation of the American Republic, 1776–1787.* Chapel Hill, N.C., 1969. This volume is helpful in acquiring an understanding of the milieu that produced the Founding Fathers.

CHAPTER 10: GEORGE MASON

Beirne, R. R., and J. H. Scarff. *William Buckland: Architect of Virginia and Maryland.* Baltimore, 1958. Tells the story of Gunston Hall, Mason's home, designed by Buckland.

Cohen, Martin B., ed. *Federalism: The Legacy of George Mason.* Fairfax, Va., 1988. A collection of four of the George Mason Lectures delivered by scholars in 1985. The second of these, "Mason Versus Madison: Developing an American Theory of Federal Democracy," delivered by Daniel J. Elazar, professor of political science and director of the Center for the Study of Federalism at Temple University, explains why Mason considered himself a federalist with a lowercase "f."

Davidow, Robert P., ed. *Natural Rights and Natural Law: The Legacy of George Mason.* Lanham, Md., 1987. Particularly relevant to Mason and religion is Michael J. Perry's essay, "The Authority of Text, Tradition, and Reason: A Theory of Constitutional Interpretation," pp. 173–246.

Grigsby, Hugh Blair. *The Virginia Convention of 1776.* Richmond, Va., 1855.

BIBLIOGRAPHY

Not always objective, but a useful account full of fascinating details.

———. *The Virginia Convention of 1788*, 2 vols. Richmond, 1890–1891. Has the same virtues as *The Virginia Convention of 1776*.

Johnson, George R., Jr., ed. *The Will of the People: The Legacy of George Mason.* Fairfax, Va. 1987. Particularly germane to appraisals of Mason's significance are Johnson's introduction and the essays "The Will of the People in Eighteenth-Century America" by Thad W. Tate and "Consensus and Pluralism: The Popular Will and the American People 1820–1940" by Alan M. Kraut.

Miller, Helen Hill. *George Mason, Constitutionalist.* Cambridge, Mass., 1938. Well researched and well written.

O'Connor, Sandra Day. *George Mason—His Lasting Influence.* Fairfax, Va., 1989. Valuable as an estimate of Mason's influence on constitutional government in the United States, an analysis written by a legal scholar who is also a U.S. Supreme Court Justice.

Rowland, Kate Mason. *Life of George Mason*, 2 vols. New York, 1892. Useful and interesting.

———. *The Life of George Mason, 1725–1792, Including His Speeches, Public Papers, and Correspondence*, 2 vols. New York, 1892. Reprint, 1964. Superseded in some respects, but still useful.

Rutland, Robert Allen. *The Birth of the Bill of Rights, 1776–1791.* Chapel Hill, N.C., 1955. A leading Mason scholar effectively explains Mason's role in the writing of the Bill of Rights and the protection of American liberties. Presents Mason's interaction with fellow delegates and explains his attitude toward ratification of the Constitution of the United States.

———. *George Mason: Reluctant Statesman.* Williamsburg, Va., 1961. Sound and concise.

Wood, Gordon S. *The Creation of the American Republic, 1776–1787.* Chapel Hill, N.C., 1969. This volume is helpful in acquiring an understanding of the milieu that produced the Founding Fathers.

CHAPTER 11: CHARLES CARROLL OF CARROLLTON

Dear Papa, Dear Charley, by Ronald Hofmann, is by far the fullest and liveliest account of the Maryland patriot. The subtitle displays the work's comprehensiveness as well as its lively interest in many a propos subjects: *The Peregrination of a Revolutionary Aristocrat as Told by Charles Carroll of Carrollton and his father, Charles Carroll of Annapolis, with sundry observations on bastardy, child-rearing, romance, matrimony, commerce, tobacco, slavery, and the politics of Revolutionary America.* The foundation of the work is the correspondence between the two Charles Carrolls, father and son. The tale told is one likely to excite incredulity succeeded by whetted curiosity.

In preparation of this chapter, I benefited from discussions with Ron Hofmann and his chief assisstant, Sally Mason, as well as from reading their work. Together they have done more to collect and publicize fresh information on Charles Carroll than have the biographers of any other signer.

Other works have been helpful:

Hanley, Thomas O'Brien. *The Making of a Revolutionary Gentleman.* Washington, D.C., 1970; Chicago, 1982.

Mason, Kate Rowland. *The Life of Charles Carroll of Carrollton, 1737-1832, with His Correspondence and Public Papers.* New York, 1898.

Smith, Ellen Hart. *Charles Carroll of Carrollton.* Cambridge, Mass., 1942. A visit to Charles Carroll's well-preserved home in Annapolis also provides glimpses of his patriarchal lifestyle.

CHAPTER 12: HAYM SALOMON

Barnard, Harry. *The Great Triumvirate of Patriots*, Chicago, 1971. Presents in chapters 8–15 a good summary of America's financial woes in the Revolution and the ability and devotion with which Salomon addressed them.

Baron, H. S. *Haym Salomon: Immigrant and Financier of the American Revolution.* Bloch, N.Y., 1929. Fictionalized account of Salomon's life, but includes much documentation in pp. 60–103.

Friedman, Lee M. *Jewish Pioneers and Patriots.* Philadelphia, 1942.

Grinstein, Hyman B., ed. and trans. "Haym Salomon Letter to Rabbi David Tevele Schiff, London, 1784." *Publications of the American Jewish Historical Society*, n.d. Not filled with personal revelations, but one of the few authenticated letters by Salomon affording a glimpse of personal concerns.

Hart, Charles Spencer. *General Washington's Son of Israel and Other Forgotten Heroes of History.* Philadelphia, 1937. The title is misleading. In this work of 229 pages, only the first 19 are about Salomon. Though the account is undocumented, it is essentially accurate, especially in its narration of American neglect. Incidentally, it also introduces many readers to such neglected figures as William Dawes, Sam Davis, Johnny Fitch, Amerigo Vespucci, J. A. McGahan, and Squire Boone.

Hutchinson, W. T., and W. M. Rachal, eds. *The Papers of James Madison*, vols. 4 and 5. Chicago, 1967.

Morais, Henry Samuel. *The Jews of Philadelphia: Their History from the Earliest Settlements to the Present Time: A Record of Events and Institutions, and Leading Members of the Jewish Community in Every Sphere of Activity.* Philadelphia, 1894. Places Haym Salomon in the context of his community and co-religionists. Particularly useful in this regard are chapters III and IV, pp. 15–30.

Patriot's Foundation of Chicago. *The Story of the George Washington, Robert*

BIBLIOGRAPHY

Morris, Haym Salomon Monument with the Proceedings at the Unveiling Dedication December 15, 1941, the One Hundred Fiftieth Anniversary of the Ratification of the Bill of Rights. The Patriot's Foundation of Chicago, 1942. Quotations from such prominent Americans as Presidents William Howard Taft, Calvin Coolidge, and Herbert Hoover and Vice President Alben W. Barkley, together with editorials from three major newspapers, reflect American attitudes toward Salomon.

Peters, Madison C. *The Jews Who Stood by Washington: An Unwritten Chapter in American History.* New York, 1915. Information on Salomon's family and on his descendants' efforts to establish proof of his services.

Russell, Charles Edward. *Haym Salomon and the Revolution.* New York, 1930. Clearly summarizes and documents much evidence supporting the value of Salomon to the Revolutionary cause.

Schwartz, Laurens R. *Jews and the American Revolution: Haym Salomon and Others.* Jefferson, N.C., 1987. A documented account of Salomon's life in the context of the Jewish community. Documentation includes nine photographs of relevant documents.

Shapiro, Michael. *The Jewish 100: A Ranking of the Most Influential Jews of All Time.* London, 1997. The author argues that Salomon deserves recognition as one of the one hundred most influential Jews in world history.

Sparks, Jared. "A Sketch of Haym Salomon," annotated by J. H. Hollander and printed in *Publications of the American Jewish Historical Society*, vol. 2. Baltimore, 1894, pp. 5–19. Sparks was a distinguished professor of history at Harvard University and possessed memoranda from the Salomon family. The manuscript offers impressive evidence of the value and extent of Haym Salomon's services to his adopted country.

Sterling, Robert T. "Haym Salomon: Forgotten Man of the Revolution," *Panorama* 18, no. 7 (1976).

Sumner, William Graham. *The Financier and the Finances of the American Revolution*, 2 vols. New York, 1891. Not important as a source of information specifically on Haym Salomon, but on Robert Morris, the Founding Father with whom he worked most closely, and on financial conditions in America during the Revolution, including the governmental apparatus set up to deal with money problems. Sumner, a professor of political and social science at Yale University, was well prepared for the task of authorship.

Wolf, Edwin, and Maxwell Whiteman. *The History of the Jews of Philadelphia from Colonial Times to the Age of Jackson.* Philadelphia, 1956. Places Salomon in the context of co-religionists and fellow citizens of Philadelphia.

Wood, Gordon S. *The Creation of the American Republic, 1776–1787.* Chapel Hill, N.C., 1969. This volume is helpful in acquiring an understanding of the milieu that produced the Founding Fathers.

Index

University of Virginia, 21

Valley Forge, 67
Virgil, 57
Virginia, 42, 45, 47-49, 74, 86-87, 94-95,
    112, 119-121, 152
Virginia Association, 116
Virginia Baptist Association, 44
Virginia Bill of Rights of 1776, 48, 117
Virginia Constitutional Convention of
    1776, 42, 48, 117
Virginia Declaration of Rights, 120
Virginia Gazette, 44
Virginia General Assembly, 94
Virginia House of Delegates, 48
Virginia Magazine of History and Biography, 121
Virginia Plan, 49
Virginia Statute for Religious Freedom,
    7-9, 21, 22, 49, 94, 158-160
Voltaire, 29, 35, 46

Washington, George, 42, 66-79, 97, 102-
    103, 115, 152, 155-156

Washington, George Augustine, 70
Washington, Lawrence, 71
Washington family, 113
Weatherford, Rev. John, 94
Weems, Mason Locke, 67
Westover, 88
Wharton, Charles W., 144
Whatley, George, 39
Whitefield, George, 154
Whitehead, Alfred North, 11, 157
Wilde, Oscar, 99
Williams, Roger, 28
Williamsburg, Va., 4, 44, 71, 90, 112, 156
Winchester, Va., 80
Winchester Republican, 81
Witherspoon, John, 44, 46, 101
Wordsworth, William, 123
Wormley family, 113
Wythe, George, 4, 5

Yorktown, Va., 99

About the Author

ALF J. MAPP, JR. meticulously researched and colorfully written books and articles have circled the globe in nine languages. Most famous of his ten volumes are *Thomas Jefferson: A Strange Case of Mistaken Identity* and *Thomas Jefferson: Passionate Pilgrim*, both of which were featured selections of the Book-of-the-Month Club and best sellers. His published articles have ranged from the *New York Times* and *Wall Street Journal* to learned journals and encyclopedias.

His writings have won him a place on the Ten Best List of the American History Publications Society, a Freedoms Foundation Honor Medal, and inclusion in the American Bicentennial Institute file of "Molders of American Culture." In a public ceremony in the State Capitol, he was made a Commonwealth of Virginia Cultural Laureate.

In more than thirty years at Old Dominion University, where he taught classes in history, literature, creative writing, and western civilization, he was twice honored with the Outstanding American Educator Award. He now bears from the university the titles Eminent Scholar Emeritus and Louis I. Jaffe Chair Emeritus.

Writing, lecturing, and guest appearances on television and radio keep him busy. He lives with his wife, Ramona, in Portsmouth, Virginia on the Elizabeth River on land first surveyed by Captain John Smith in 1608.

AUG   2016

CPSIA information can be obtained
at www.ICGtesting.com
Printed in the USA
FSOW03n2139030816
23425FS